Lloyd C. Russow
Editor

Digital Technology in Teaching International Business

Digital Technology in Teaching International Business has been co-published simultaneously as *Journal of Teaching in International Business*, Volume 14, Numbers 2/3 2003.

Pre-publication REVIEWS, COMMENTARIES, EVALUATIONS . . .

"MUST READING . . . A VALUABLE RESOURCE GUIDE for those wanting to learn more about the daunting challenges of using the Internet in teaching international business. . . . Provides valuable insights into the benefits and pitfalls of using computer-mediated communication systems, particularly when student participants are spread across national borders and time. . . . Provides several case studies of successful collaborative distance learning projects between colleges in the United States and developing/emerging nations."

Anthony C. Koh, PhD
Interim Chair and Associate Professor
Department of International Business
Entrepreneurship, and Strategy
College of Business Administration
The University of Toledo

More pre-publication
REVIEWS, COMMENTARIES, EVALUATIONS . . .

"HIGHLY RECOMMENDED. . . . An excellent collection. . . . Presents the pros and cons of the digitization of education. . . . Provides a balanced view of online education . . . detailed insights and analysis regarding this hot topic. The virtue of Professor Russow's book is that it is not dogmatic. It is a rich collection of thoughts and experiences from a variety of faculty members involved in online education at different universities."

Jaideep T. Naidu, PhD
Assistant Professor
School of Business Administration
Philadelphia University

"TIMELY . . . EXCELLENT . . . ENGAGING. . . . A must-read for institutions and academics using the Internet to enhance the dissemination of information and to enrich the global experience of their students. The authors explore how technology can be successfully used to bridge the distance between countries and cultures, professors and students, and corporations and classrooms."

Philip S. Russel, PhD
Assistant Professor of Finance
School of Business Administration
Philadelphia

IBP

International Business Press
An Imprint of The Haworth Press, Inc.

Digital Technology in Teaching International Business

Digital Technology in Teaching International Business has been co-published simultaneously as *Journal of Teaching in International Business*, Volume 14, Numbers 2/3 2003.

The *Journal of Teaching in International Business* Monographic "Separates"

Below is a list of "separates," which in serials librarianship means a special issue simultaneously published as a special journal issue or double-issue *and* as a "separate" hardbound monograph. (This is a format which we also call a "DocuSerial.")

"Separates" are published because specialized libraries or professionals may wish to purchase a specific thematic issue by itself in a format which can be separately cataloged and shelved, as opposed to purchasing the journal on an on-going basis. Faculty members may also more easily consider a "separate" for classroom adoption.

"Separates" are carefully classified separately with the major book jobbers so that the journal tie-in can be noted on new book order slips to avoid duplicate purchasing.

You may wish to visit Haworth's website at . . .

http://www.HaworthPress.com

. . . to search our online catalog for complete tables of contents of these separates and related publications.

You may also call 1-800-HAWORTH (outside US/Canada: 607-722-5857), or Fax 1-800-895-0582 (outside US/Canada: 607-771-0012), or e-mail at:

getinfo@haworthpress.com

Digital Technology in Teaching International Business, edited by Lloyd C. Russow (Vol. 14, No. 2/3, 2003). *"VERY TIMELY . . . A MUST-READ . . . Provides real-world applications of digital instruction in international business. (Sam C. Okoroafo, PhD, Professor of International Business, University of Toledo; Editor,"* Journal of African Business)

International Business Teaching in Eastern and Central European Countries, edited by George Tesar (Vol. 13, No. 3/4, 2002). *"Important . . . Offers unique and current insights." (Jerome K. Laurent, PhD, Professor of Economics, University of Wisconsin-Whitewater)*

Management Education in the Chinese Setting, edited by Alma Whiteley (Vol. 12, No. 2, 2001). *"Explores the challenges and opportunities that Greater China offers to educators in program and course development, delivery of programs and other materials, and the development of instructors."*

Teaching International Business: Ethics and Corporate Social Responsibility, edited by Gopalkrishnan R. Iyer (Vol. 11, No. 1, 1999). *"This book is a collection of academic writings on the issues and challenges of incorporating ethics and corporate social responsibility concerns into international business education. You will find frameworks and approaches detailing various pedagogical issues presented."*

Teaching and Program Variations in International Business, edited by Erdener Kaynak and John R. Schermerhorn, Jr. (Vol. 10, No. 3/4, 1999). *"This informative guide explores new avenues that will assist educators in providing undergraduate and graduate students with important, firsthand experiences in international business. Becoming competitive in today's global market is increasingly difficult, and this book will help you use organizational learning tools, the Internet, and agency accreditations to fully prepare students for a successful career in the international marketplace."*

Business Simulations, Games and Experiential Learning in International Business Education, edited by Joseph Wolfe and J. Bernard Keys (Vol. 8, No. 4, 1997). *"A concise and useful collection of materials that might be used to enhance the effectiveness of international business games and simulations." (Saeed Samiee, Professor of Marketing, College of Business Administration, The University of Tulsa, Tulsa, OK)*

The Teaching of Organizational Behavior Across Discipline and National Boundaries: A Role for Information Technology, edited by Alma M. Whiteley (Vol. 7, No. 4, 1996). *"Makes an important contribution to the teaching of organizational behavior by contributing to our understanding of the process by which the effectiveness can be enhanced by group processes, both in educational and strategy development contexts. This is a text for the bookshelf of every business school teacher irrespective of discipline." (David McHardy Reid, PhD, Director, Citicorp Doctoral Programme, School of Business, University of Hong Kong)*

Central and Eastern Europe and the CIS, edited by Jerome Witt (Vol. 7, No. 2, 1996). *"A good overview of the problems of Western-generated reform efforts to business and economic education in the transnational economies of Central and Eastern Europe and the CIS." (Earl Molander, Professor, School of Business Administration, Portland State University)*

Internationalization of the Business Curriculum, edited by Manton C. Gibbs, Jr. (Vol. 5, No. 3, 1994). *"A timely masterpiece which is one step ahead of other books of its kind. . . . Invaluable for university administrators, faculty and business students, industry practitioners, corporate planners, and policymakers." (Jaideep Motwani, PhD, Assistant Professor of Management, Grand Valley State University)*

Environmental Issues in the Curricula of International Business: The Green Imperative, edited by Alma T. Mintu-Wimsatt, Héctor R. Lozada, and Michael J. Polonsky (Vol. 5, No. 1/2, 1994). *"One of the first attempts to make international business academics aware of environmental issues. . . . Contains interdisciplinary information that will appeal to a diverse audience including researchers, practitioners, policymakers, and students." (Journal of Asian Business)*

Utilizing New Information Technology in Teaching of International Business: A Guide for Instructors, edited by Fahri Karakaya and Erdener Kaynak (Vol. 4, No. 3/4, 1993). *"Concise . . . This volume offers a series of evaluators of the latest computer information techniques and tools with an eye to their utility as teaching tools . . . written from a user's perspective. . . . Offers the instructor quick access to information about the new information technologies available." (Ronald S. Rubin, Professor of Marketing, University of Central Florida)*

Published by

International Business Press®, 10 Alice Street, Binghamton, NY 13904-1580 USA

International Business Press® is an imprint of The Haworth Press, Inc., 10 Alice Street, Binghamton, NY 13904-1580 USA.

Digital Technology in Teaching International Business has been co-published simultaneously as *Journal of Teaching in International Business*, Volume 14, Numbers 2/3 2003.

The Haworth Press, Inc., 10 Alice Street, Binghamton, NY 13904-1580 USA

Cover design by Marylouise E. Doyle

Library of Congress Cataloging-in-Publication Data

Digital technology in teaching international business / Lloyd C. Russow, editor.
p. cm.
"Digital Technology in Teaching International Business has been co-published simultaneously as Journal of Teaching in International Business, Volume 14, Numbers 2/3 2003."
Includes bibliographical references (p.) and index.
ISBN 0-7890-2062-9 (hard)–ISBN 0-7890-2063-7 (pbk.)
1. Business education–Computer-assisted instruction. I. Russow, Lloyd C. II. Journal of teaching in international business.
HF1106 .D54 2002
658' .049'0785–dc21

2002151054

Digital Technology in Teaching International Business

Lloyd C. Russow, PhD
Editor

Digital Technology in Teaching International Business has been co-published simultaneously as *Journal of Teaching in International Business*, Volume 14, Numbers 2/3 2003.

International Business Press
An Imprint of
The Haworth Press, Inc.
New York • London • Oxford

Indexing, Abstracting & Website/Internet Coverage

This section provides you with a list of major indexing & abstracting services. That is to say, each service began covering this periodical during the year noted in the right column. Most Websites which are listed below have indicated that they will either post, disseminate, compile, archive, cite or alert their own Website users with research-based content from this work. (This list is as current as the copyright date of this publication.)

Abstracting, Website/Indexing Coverage	Year When Coverage Began
• *Business Education Index, The*	1993
• *CNPIEC Reference Guide: Chinese National Directory of Foreign Periodicals*	1996
• *Contents Pages in Education*	1992
• *Education Process Improvement Ctr, Inc (EPICENTER) <http://www.epicent.com>*	1999
• *Educational Technology Abstracts*	1992
• *ERIC: Current Index to Journals in Education*	1998
• *FINDEX <www.publist.com>*	1999
• *IBZ International Bibliography of Periodical Literature*	1996
• *Index to Periodical Articles Related to Law*	1992
• *International Bulletin of Bibliography on Education*	1992

(continued)

- ***Management & Marketing Abstracts*** **1992**
- ***Multicultural Education Abstracts*** **1999**
- ***Resources in Education (RIE)*** **1995**
- ***School Organisation & Management Abstracts*** **1990**
- ***Special Education Needs Abstracts*** **1990**
- ***Technical Education & Training Abstracts*** **1992**

Special Bibliographic Notes related to special journal issues (separates) and indexing/abstracting:

- indexing/abstracting services in this list will also cover material in any "separate" that is co-published simultaneously with Haworth's special thematic journal issue or DocuSerial. Indexing/abstracting usually covers material at the article/chapter level.
- monographic co-editions are intended for either non-subscribers or libraries which intend to purchase a second copy for their circulating collections.
- monographic co-editions are reported to all jobbers/wholesalers/approval plans. The source journal is listed as the "series" to assist the prevention of duplicate purchasing in the same manner utilized for books-in-series.
- to facilitate user/access services all indexing/abstracting services are encouraged to utilize the co-indexing entry note indicated at the bottom of the first page of each article/chapter/contribution.
- this is intended to assist a library user of any reference tool (whether print, electronic, online, or CD-ROM) to locate the monographic version if the library has purchased this version but not a subscription to the source journal.
- individual articles/chapters in any Haworth publication are also available through the Haworth Document Delivery Service (HDDS).

ALL INTERNATIONAL BUSINESS PRESS
BOOKS AND JOURNALS ARE PRINTED
ON CERTIFIED ACID-FREE PAPER

Digital Technology in Teaching International Business

CONTENTS

ABOUT THE EDITOR

Lloyd C. Russow, PhD, is Associate Professor of International Business and Marketing and Associate Dean of the School of Business Administration at Philadelphia University. Dr. Russow has published numerous articles and books on international business and marketing. His Everything International Web site (http://international-business.info) has been cited as one of the top five international trade sites in the world by Lycos, and is referenced by publishers, libraries, and universities around the world.

Dr. Russow has taught online and has been using various digital technologies in his traditional classes since 1995. He established and is responsible for distance learning in the School of Business Administration at Philadelphia University where he manages the curriculum and faculty for all courses currently being offered online. Dr. Russow is also an invited speaker by professional and academic groups on topics related to Internet research and online teaching techniques.

Digitization of Education: A Panacea?

Lloyd C. Russow

Let's replace the outmoded physical plant of the world's universities with virtual universities that concentrate on learning, rather than maintaining a pretty campus with athletic stadiums, faculty lounges, dining rooms and classrooms. Everyone in the world can now learn about the most effective management techniques, anytime, anywhere. Education on demand; just-in-time knowledge. Get rid of the sage on the stage and put in its place the guide on the side. Substitute the chalk and talk with the discussion thread. Digitize all the books, journals and databases and turn our mammoth libraries into something more useful. Do all this and the world will be a better place where cheap and easy access to education is available to all!

A noble thought where ALL people have equal access to the same knowledge, where someone is limited only by their own motivation to learn. Can new technology free us to do this? This is one question asked, and in some cases, partly answered by the research that follows. The conclusion is that for now at least, faculty and the bricks-and-mortar institutions will be around for some time to come. Things will look a little different, and learning may take place in very different ways, but these institutions will not be replaced by the virtual university and an army of guides and assistants.

Lloyd C. Russow is Associate Professor of International Business and Marketing and Associate Dean of the School of Business Administration, Philadelphia University, School House Lane and Henry Avenue, Philadelphia, PA 19144-5497.

[Haworth co-indexing entry note]: "Digitization of Education: A Panacea?" Russow, Lloyd C. Co-published simultaneously in *Journal of Teaching in International Business* (International Business Press, an imprint of The Haworth Press, Inc.) Vol. 14, No. 2/3, 2003, pp. 1-11; and: *Digital Technology in Teaching International Business* (ed: Lloyd C. Russow) International Business Press, an imprint of The Haworth Press, Inc., 2003, pp. 1-11. Single or multiple copies of this article are available for a fee from The Haworth Document Delivery Service [1-800-HAWORTH 9:00 a.m. - 5:00 p.m. (EST). E-mail address: getinfo@haworthpress.com].

One can state that education is more accessible because of new technologies. Perhaps the more important issue, though, is the ability of poorer countries to catch-up with the developed nations. The knowledge gap is widening at a dizzying pace because those that have (access to computers and the Internet infrastructure) are constantly upgrading and those that have not must still concentrate on housing, health, and other issues that are key to their survival, and cannot be concerned whether the few computers they DO have run on Windows 3.1 or Windows XP. Despite the best efforts the World Bank Global Development Learning Network <http://www.gldin.org> and heroic government efforts like that taking place in Brazil, the gap will widen in the near and medium-term future. Wide differences in education means widening differences in income and overall well being, which in turn exacerbates political stability.

Is it accurate to believe that education will be free, or even get cheaper in real terms? Again the euphoria about new technologies may be misleading. Yes, we have access to information for less money. Consider, for example how many magazine subscriptions you can afford. How many periodicals are available online free-of-charge? How many service providers offer their services in exchange for information about you? That's free too, isn't it? As we learn the cost of converting our classes to web-based or Internet-enhanced versions, and as we learn that we can't handle hundreds of online students because of the increased communication demands, the realization is that the cost of education will not decrease, it may actually increase. This is reflected in articles one reads in the *Chronicle of Higher Education*, popular press, as well as academic journal articles.

The time needed to prepare and teach online courses is much more than with a traditional class, not only because we must learn how best to use the technologies ourselves, but because of the tremendous increase in communications with our students. While increased individualized communication can only improve the learning experience, it does have associated costs–smaller "classrooms." Many faculty can stand before a class of 80 and lecture. It is doubtful that the same faculty could handle an online class of 30, let alone 80 students, even if the instructor uses associated faculty. Faculty and institutions are grappling with tough intellectual property questions that may end in providing additional compensation for development of digital teaching tools. These expenses will be passed on to the consumer.

Add to these costs that textbook publishers have been consolidating which means less competition and perhaps higher prices for the same goods. These larger firms are now issuing pin numbers, bundled into the price of the texts, which allow students temporary access to Internet materials. Software manufacturers like Microsoft have devised new methods of protecting their software, making it more difficult to copy and rightly (from the developed nation perspective) making it more expensive for people in developing nations to gain access to the software needed to run the online education systems. As more firms realize they cannot survive on advertising income alone, fewer publications and services are available for free. How can stay-at-home students, or even small and medium-sized firms afford to spend the money necessary to maintain the latest hardware, software and infrastructure necessary for students to learn about them? Someone must pay for these, whether the large educational facility, the large firm, or the wealthy individual student. Again, cost issues will widen the gap between the people of poorer and richer nations. Education may be cheaper, but only marginally so in real terms.

The physical plant of the university fulfills a critical role in education today. Without the university, we would again be faced with a situation where only the elite would be educated. Only the richest of households are able to keep up with the hardware and software that are necessary to take advantage of the latest technologies. Schools provide and more importantly maintain the computer laboratories and infrastructure that only a very few can afford to develop on their own. Assuming they maintain apace of new technologies, institutions of higher learning provide ALL students who attend the opportunity to learn how to apply the latest technologies in situations they are likely to confront once they graduate. Over the past century, we as a society have made access to universities easier and more affordable to those living in developed and developing nations alike.

Whether in traditional classrooms or online format, the tools needed to participate in online learning, especially at the fringes where streaming video, students participating in team development of term projects through shared server space, and other innovative practices all require the latest in hardware and software. While costs are coming down continuously, the cost of the high-end equipment and the latest software necessary to take advantage of these technologies remain and will continue to remain in the thousands of dollars. This also doesn't consider that schools' libraries provide access to electronic and non-electronic materials that students cannot afford to purchase on their own. This can easily be verified. People who can afford to upgrade their software and hardware at least every three years could likely "keep up." But, try using a machine that is five years old with software of the same age in an online course. A good portion of that course would be inaccessible.

Perhaps in the medium-term (10, 15, or 20 years), we as a society can make it affordable to attend virtual universities too. But to believe that the Internet makes education accessible to all, regardless of income, and that the real cost of education will fall dramatically because of these new technologies may be woefully inaccurate, at least within the short-term. Large institutions or organizations can spread the costs of acquiring the needed tools over a large audience and we cannot shift that burden, or expect that individuals are capable of underwriting a substantial portion of that in the short-term.

It is doubtful that with today's technology, education will be available to everyone on demand. We have discovered some tools that make education more affordable, more accessible, and richer in many cases. Yet, the message that comes from the research in this issue is that we should proceed with open minds and we should be prepared to take on some rather large and perplexing social issues that will arise from the digitization of education.

The first article by Professors Benbunan-Fich and Stoever reviews the literature on Computer-Mediated Communication Systems (CMCS) applied to teaching and learning and examines the implications for international business (IB) education. The authors present a framework to classify the different strategies for improving case study discussion with the use of Computer-Mediated Communications and enriching such discussions with the integration of different cultural perspectives.

CMCS can be used to support the administrative type of communication that take place in a course and/or to transmit course content. As a communications-support tool, IT can be used to extend the availability of the professors beyond office hours and to accomplish administrative activities such as distribution of materials, reminders and notifications. As a content-transmission tool, these systems can complement or completely replace the traditional role of textbook and teachers. The article addresses the use of this technology to promote discussion of IB cases among participants from different countries and cultures; it could of course be extended to other types of cases and other pedagogical applications.

At an operational level, CMCS can promote more interactive learning for participants from objectivist traditions by removing or at least reducing feelings of awkwardness, reluctance to challenge authority figures such as course instructors, and cultural inhibitions against disagreeing with colleagues or acquaintances. They can also enhance performance of cross-cultural and cross-national groups, due in part to the visibility that the system can provide to each response, combined with deeper reflection in asynchronous work. Thus they can aid in narrowing of the gap between objectivist and constructivist approaches to case learning.

There can also be a reverse benefit, however: participants schooled in constructivist approaches may gain more understanding of the thinking and behaviors of participants from objectivist backgrounds and may thus improve their own abilities to interact and reach agreement with their opposite numbers. Thus Western-educated participants may come to appreciate the unique perspectives and contributions that persons from non-Western educational traditions can offer.

Next, Cliff Wymbs and Hugo Kijne present a discussion on the dilemma between richness and reach when using digital technology in teaching international business. The use of the Internet has the potential to greatly affect the reach of teaching International Business (courses can be taught across continents) and dramatically improve the richness (students can be exposed to cross-cultural negotiations and problem solving). The unique aspects of international business, i.e., sensitivity to culture, exposure to diverse political regimes, complex behavioral interactions, make it an ideal candidate for technological experimentation by the academic community. They discuss how students can use the Internet as a medium to personally participate in international problem solving exercises. Students who use this approach to gain a good appreciation of foreign cognitive, affective and behavioral patterns will be in a better position to become future international business leaders. The challenge is how to use technology to accomplish this goal.

The authors argue that teachers of international business are well aware of the problems and opportunities associated with teaching subject matter that is geographically remote. In response to this, a limited number of expensive programs have been developed to give students rich individual experiences associated with foreign travel. Only recently has Internet technology been used to increase the availability and reduce the cost of interactive programs connecting students from geographically dispersed locations. Their analysis extends the traditional marketing tradeoffs between richness (depth of knowledge) and reach (geographic area coverage) to the emerging technology-mediated education industry, and then evaluates their effect on the teaching of international business.

This article identifies various approaches being used to teach international business and provides evaluations of each along richness and reach dimensions. The authors suggest that a logical next step is to do survey research and test how students and faculty evaluate each alternative along consistent learning objectives and preferences and to specifically evaluate the richness and reach attributes.

The third article, "Transforming Educational and Business Practices in Belarus: Collaborative Learning at a Distance" by Drs. Langlois, Litoff, and Ilacqua presents an initiative spearheaded by Bryant College that uses Internet technologies to advance change in educational values, communication competencies, and business practices in Belarus and other republics of the former Soviet Union. Bryant College led a Collaborative Learning at a Distance (CLD) Program involving the European Humanities University (EHU) and the ENVILA Institute for Women in Minsk, a Summer School in Minsk on Collaborative Learning at a Distance, and a Rhode Island-based internship Center for International Collaboration (CIC) at the Information Technologies Center (ITC) of the National Academy of Sciences of Belarus.

An interactive, non-hierarchical model of learning was utilized throughout the CLD Program, enabling faculty, students, scientists, technicians, entrepreneurs, and non-governmental organizations (NGO) leaders to collaborate in the creation of new pathways for communication and creative problem solving. A faculty exchange component was employed to enhance collaboration, heighten commitment to ongoing projects, and to observe firsthand the results of the program activities. A Summer School, designed to broaden Internet skills and orient faculty to Web-based educational tools, was held in Minsk.

Direct interaction with young entrepreneurs and NGO managers has been provided through an ongoing Community Connections Business Program, with follow-up site visits and post-program seminars in Minsk. Future activities will include the development of learning modules for business practitioners, and the utilization of the CIC to integrate classroom experience, broad-based distance learning projects, and business training throughout the NIS.

Underlying all the projects associated with the Bryant/Belarus CLD Program is a commitment to collaborative approaches to problem solving and decision making that takes into account cross-cultural challenges. At this point, it appears that Internet-enhanced courses and training programs focused on collaborative learning provide practical opportunities for academic, business, and research decision makers from the NIS to address local and regional challenges, and to participate more fully in global markets.

The next article, "Preparing the Human Capital for the New Millennium Using Information Technology" by D. K. and Rashmi Malhotra, points out that the continued growth of information technology has tremendous impact on today's global businesses and the need for workers who can manage a vast amount of information. The authors state that information technology is transforming the economy at a breathtaking speed and that the effect of technology on global business practices is profound and pervasive. Furthermore, these trends are changing and shaping the global economic landscape in the new millennium. These developments have major implications for the knowledge skills required for success in business in the information age. Students must be prepared for the challenges and opportunities that each of these trends represents. Therefore, they argue, the new knowledge economy demands changes in the models of global business education.

Businesses need employees who recognize problems and use information technology to solve business problems. As we enter the new millennium, it is time to re-evaluate the materials and methods educators use to prepare business students for success in the global workplace. International integration, innovations in information technology, mass customization, and the diversification of the American labor force continue to shape the landscape of tomorrow. This article outlines the challenges and demands of the knowledge-based economy, and discusses the path universities should follow in providing business students with the skills they need to succeed in this complex environment. Further, the authors illustrate their experiences in dealing with the advances in Information Technology from three major viewpoints–a general impact of information technology on business education, developing IT-infused curriculum, and the major rewards and challenges posed to universities. The fifth article, by Dr. Ilan Alon begins with the premise that dramatic changes have taken place in business education over the last two decades, primarily because of technological innovations and globalization. The Internet has facilitated the free flow of communication and the dissemination of information with little regard for national boundaries. Internet technologies have impacted business education in a variety of ways. At the same time, the last couple of decades have seen an explosion in international trade, international investment, and cross-border alliances. The virtual global village allows participants to emerge from remote corners of the world and interact with investors and educators alike.

The article describes the implementation of Internet-based experiential projects within an international-business classroom setting and summarizes students' perceptions and attitudes towards the assignments. It tests the effectiveness of using an Internet-based experiential project (<www.Globalview.org>) to augment learning outcomes in an international business class. The project has a number of advantages over traditional approaches of teaching international business:

1. It uses digital technology to communicate and disseminate information.
2. It is based on real-world–"live"–global cases.
3. It requires distributive collaborative learning.

On average, students mildly enjoyed the project with an average rating of 3.18 (on a scale of 1-5, 3.0 is a neutral position), gained an appreciation of what it takes to work in groups (3.65), developed international business skills and abilities (3.89), worked extremely hard to complete the assignment (4.10), and were slightly more productive then they would have been in a traditional lecture or project environment (3.54). The negatively worded questions were, as expected, lower than 3.0 (with an average rating of 2.36).

The project described in this paper is a proven success in terms of learning outcomes and student-reported perceptions. The companies involved benefited from international business plans that can be used to identify selected countries for expansion. The school enjoyed several benefits from its collaboration with the business community: at the very least, the program enhanced the learning environment and provided students with "real-world" skills and abilities that they should be able to reproduce for their potential employers.

Dr. Van Miller writes in the sixth article that teaching business strategy courses about developing countries represents a challenge to higher education, given its developed-country bias. As a pedagogical issue, it hardly existed ten years ago, even though four-fifths of the world's people live in developing countries or emerging economies. However, when Secretary Ron Brown coined the term "emerging economies" for use in the promotion of U.S. exports, it quickly entered into the lexicon of international business educators. To confront the challenge, a group of such educators met in the summer of 1998 to learn how faculty in the Kellogg Graduate School of Management were dealing with it via a special course and a simulation then contained on a CD but now permanently housed on a website. Based on that experience and three experiments with teaching such a course, a pedagogical structure with the key ingredients for an emerging economies strategy course is presented herein. Those key ingredients are:

a. general and specific information about the particulars of such economies
b. knowledge about the business strategy concept, and
c. a learning experience that integrates the information and the concepts. Each of the experiments conducted while teaching this course either omitted or included these ingredients in the quest to construct an integrative course that would satisfy the challenge for a business strategy course relevant to the developing countries.

Van Miller shows that the experiments do not demonstrate definitively that the Simulation is a superior teaching tool. While computer-aided technologies may enhance student learning about the technology, it does not seem to be the case with respect to the substance of the course. Dr. Miller shows that the technology clearly has appeal to the students, but its efficacy in their learning is still a question needing an answer. Second, the Simulation is in English and its tools rely upon that language and very specific/special terms for accomplishing their purpose. Those terms must be mastered by the students to use the Simulation well. A native speaker of English can master the terminology without much trouble; however, for the user who is not fluent in English the terms become a challenge if not an obstacle. Until it is translated into other languages, this presents a real burden for those of us who desire to utilize the Simulation with students who reside in the world of real emerging economies and with the intent of assisting those economies in their development.

"Using Internet Resources in Teaching Financial Reporting and Analysis of Multinational Enterprises" by Dr. Abdel Agami is an interesting article. This article provides some sources of corporate financial information on the Internet and illustrates how to use these resources in teaching international business and, more specifically, financial reporting and analysis of multinational enterprises and to point out some of the advantages and limitations of these resources.

Professor Agami states that there has been an increase in the number and type of sources of corporate financial information on the Internet in recent years; the number of corporations that have web pages that post corporate financial information is increasing; and many government and regulatory agencies are also posting corporate financial information. Furthermore, there are some third-party sites that post corporate financial information. In recent years some software were developed or are in the process of being developed to gather, analyze, and monitor information available on the Internet to accomplish specific tasks on behalf of its users.

He argues that the use of financial information available on the Internet enriches discussion in class and provides up-to-date information relevant to the issues discussed in the course. Information available on the Internet is frequently available at no cost or at a very low cost; the Internet increases the speed of dissemination of the information; makes the use of information easier; and provides the information on a timely basis. On the other hand, information on the Internet sometimes lacks completeness; is not readily comparable from one company to another; in many cases is not prepared by experts (such as accountants); in some cases the information is not prepared according to generally accepted accounting principles; and it is not always audited by a certified public accountant. He concludes with the idea that other sources should be used to supplement Internet sources whenever it is possible.

In the last article, Cathy Rusinko states that in adapting to an online teaching environment, one of the greatest challenges in a course such as international management is adapting experiential exercises from live courses that help students to develop contextual understanding of topics such as cultural differences–particularly in an asynchronous environment.

In addition, researchers suggest that successful online courses tend to demand a change in pedagogy–from a more traditional lecture-based pedagogy where the instructor is central to the learning process, to a more collaborative, high involvement environment, where students are actively involved and the instructor is more of a facilitator in the learning process (e.g., Berger, 1999; Arbaugh, 2000a; 2000b; Volery & Lord, 2000). At the same time (and regardless of the type of classroom environment), both business curriculum experts and employers cite the need for more emphasis on helping students to enhance understanding of cultural differences, and improve communication skills and team skills (Day and Glick, 2000).

To address both the pedagogical challenges of the online environment and the demands by curriculum experts and employers, this paper proposes that instructors use literature (e.g., folktales; short stories) to develop experiential exercises for online courses in international management. Unlike some experiential tools that must be used in a live or synchronous environment, literature can also be used effectively in an asynchronous environment. That is, the use of literature (e.g., folktale; short story; novel chapter, etc.) as the backbone of an experiential exercise allows students to read and react at a time that is convenient for them.

This paper includes an example of how the folktale, "Stone Soup," can be used as an introductory exercise that experientially reveals the essence of effective international management. This folktale is particularly well-suited for the first day or week of class, since it can provide students with situational reinforcement of the importance of sensitivity to different cultures, and communication, motivation, leadership, and team building in a different culture. In addition, "Stone Soup" elicits a high level of student participation and helps to set the standard for high involvement at the start of the course.

While the use of literature in the business curriculum and in international management has been discussed (e.g., Puffer, 1986; Carney, 1994; Harrison and Akinc, 2000), the purpose of this paper is to make the case for, and to illustrate how literature is a tool that can help instructors to make a successful transition to the online environment.

In addition, use of literature in international management can help students to become better international managers. The complexity and ambiguity inherent in literature can help students to gain contextual understanding of, and identify with complicated and equivocal issues such as cultural differences. In addition, a team-oriented assignment that uses literature as its focus can enhance team and communication skills among students, and can help to create a high involvement environment.

The authors in this volume provide interesting insight and in some cases answers to these issues. They also raise many questions and highlight the need for future research and discussion about digitizing education–a good thing for the continued success of the *Journal of Teaching in International Business*!

Using Information Technology to Promote Multi-Cultural Case Teaching: A Pedagogical Framework

Raquel Benbunan-Fich
William A. Stoever

SUMMARY. Case studies are an important component of International Business (IB) courses. However, in-class discussion of case studies suffers from temporal and spatial limitations and, frequently, the limitation of being confined to a single cultural perspective. The development of new forms of Computer-Mediated Communication (such as email, chat rooms, threaded computer conferences, etc.) offers new possibilities to overcome these constraints. Synchronous (same-time) communication via chat rooms or desktop video-conferences may include participants from remote locations who otherwise would be unable to attend class sessions. Non-simultaneous (asynchronous) communication via e-mail and/or threaded discussion conferences can complement traditional in-class discussions and extend the learning environment beyond the assigned classroom meeting times. These new communication possibili-

---

Raquel Benbunan-Fich is Assistant Professor, Statistics & CIS Department, Zicklin School of Business, Baruch College, City University of New York. William A. Stoever is Professor of International Business, W. Paul Stillman School of Business, Seton Hall University, 400 South Orange Avenue, South Orange, NJ 07079 (E-mail: stoevewi@shu.edu).

Address correspondence to William A. Stoever.

[Haworth co-indexing entry note]: "Using Information Technology to Promote Multi-Cultural Case Teaching: A Pedagogical Framework." Benbunan-Fich, Raquel, and William A. Stoever. Co-published simultaneously in *Journal of Teaching in International Business* (International Business Press, an imprint of The Haworth Press, Inc.) Vol. 14, No. 2/3, 2003, pp. 13-27; and: *Digital Technology in Teaching International Business* (ed: Lloyd C. Russow) International Business Press, an imprint of The Haworth Press, Inc., 2003, pp. 13-27. Single or multiple copies of this article are available for a fee from The Haworth Document Delivery Service [1-800-HAWORTH 9:00 a.m. - 5:00 p.m. (EST). E-mail address: getinfo@haworthpress.com].

ties can enable instructors and students from different countries and zones to participate in case discussions and to enrich the cultural dimension of such discussions. This paper presents a framework to classify the different strategies for improving case study discussion with the use of Computer-Mediated Communications and enriching such discussions with the integration of different cultural perspectives.

KEYWORDS. Multi-cultural case teaching, computer-mediated communication systems

INTRODUCTION

This paper reviews the literature on Computer-Mediated Communication Systems (CMCS) applied to teaching and learning, examines the implications for international business (IB) education, and presents an integration framework. The three driving forces of this framework are the time dimension between participants in different countries, their geographical dispersion, and the differing perspectives of participants from different cultures. These three factors will enable us to develop a new model to create pedagogically effective environments to leverage IB education.

The increasing popularity and user-capabilities of CMCS have stimulated a large number of articles in the academic literature focusing on CMCS applications to educational activities (e.g., Benbunan-Fich & Hiltz, 1999; Scott et al., 1999; Alavi et al., 1997; Althaus, 1997; Hiltz & Wellman, 1997; LaRose et al. 1998; Smith, 1997; Webster & Hackley, 1997; Klass & Whiteley, 1996). In addition, the diffusion of the telecommunication infrastructure offers many opportunities to extend learning activities beyond the classroom. For example, CMCS are linking individual students with their peers and instructors (Hiltz, 1994), and also entire schools with their counterparts in other locations (Perrone et al., 1996; Wheeler et al., 1995).

CMCS can be used to support the administrative type of communication that take place in a course and/or to transmit course content. As a communications-support tool, IT can be used to extend the availability of the professors beyond office hours and to accomplish administrative activities such as distribution of materials, reminders and notifications. As a content-transmission tool, these systems can complement or completely replace the traditional role of textbook and teachers. Thus, CMCS can support entire courses or specific assignments such as the discussion and solution of case studies (Benbunan-Fich & Hiltz, 1999).

This paper addresses the use of this technology to promote discussion of IB cases among participants from different countries and cultures; it could of course be extended to other types of cases and other pedagogical applications. The paper is structured as follows: the next section reviews the basic teaching/learning paradigms; the third section describes different applications of CMCS to support case study discussion; the fourth presents the framework; and the last section presents the conclusions.

LEARNING PARADIGMS

Different learning strategies and activities will suggest different approaches to the use of technology-based interactions in IB education. Pedagogy-based collaborative learning will require a technological platform that supports the necessary level of communication among participants.

One way of categorizing the process of student learning is by comparing the objectivist and constructivist archetypes or models.[1] The objectivist model assumes that there is an objective reality and that the goal of learning is to understand that reality and modify one's behavior accordingly. This model is based upon a one-way or professor-centered model of knowledge transmission, in which each student learns by passively receiving and assimilating knowledge individually, independent from others (Bouton and Garth, 1983). The professor is viewed as having attained a high degree of understanding and knowledge in a particular subject by virtue of years of experience, research and study. This model is often thought to underlie the instructional methods of traditional cultures (Pisani, 2000; Parhizgar, 1998). Whitely (1996) discusses management education in Hong Kong as taking place "in a learning world where almost anything offered by the 'teacher' is perceived as erudite and appropriate." May (1997), citing Taggert et al. (1994), says " . . . the Chinese expect a structured environment wherein the teacher is guiding and directing rather than facilitating learning through group discussions or projects."

By contrast, the constructivist model assumes that knowledge is created or constructed by each learner interacting with others (Leidner and Jarvenpaa, 1995). It postulates that learning is most effective when the student is an active participant in individual or group activities. For this reason, collaborative or group learning is one of the most important implementations of the constructivist approach. Collaborative learning involves interpersonal processes whereby a small group of students work together to complete an academic problem-solving task that promotes learning. As a generalization, twentieth-century Western educational approaches tend to be based on constructivist models (Parhizgar, 1998).

We propose that the teaching and learning approaches in most cultures lie somewhere on a continuum between the objectivist and constructivist models:

objectivist <--- | | | | | | | | | | | | | ---> *constructivist*

We further propose that the appropriate use of CMC-based educational methods can help bridge the gap between the very different instructional approaches implied by these two models. The teaching and learning of IB, which by its very nature tends to be eclectic and cross-cultural, can be particularly enriched by the use of these methods. IB courses are appropriate settings for collaborative learning activities such as case study discussions, debates, group projects, negotiation exercises, simulation and role-playing exercises–the very types of pedagogy that are most richly enhanced by computer-mediated approaches (Alavi, 1994; Galegher and Kraut, 1994).

CASE STUDIES AND CMC-BASED DISCUSSIONS

Case studies are the hallmark of Western business education, especially in the United States. The case approach seeks to enable students to process instructional inputs and assimilate course materials (Leidner & Fuller, 1996). The rationale is the need to bridge the gap between the "academic goal of knowing and the practitioner's necessity of acting" (Barnes et al., 1994). The case approach is most effective in transmitting both content and real-life experiences when it achieves maximum student involvement (Leidner & Jarvenpaa, 1995). "The spirit of the methodology mandates people reacting to each other and learning through the synergies of conversation" (Hashim et al., 1991). Cases achieve this involvement when they present real or hypothetical situations that invite group discussion and the use of concepts to develop recommendations or achieve preferred solutions (Barnes et al., 1994; Benbunan-Fich, 1997; Hashim et al., 1991; Silver et al., 1995). Most IB courses are appropriate environments for the use of case studies.

Participation in discussions is the crucial element to learning by the case method. However, individuals even from Western cultures may be reluctant to participate in face-to-face discussions for a number of reasons, including fear of reprisals, fear of being evaluated or mocked by peers, fragmentation of available speaking time, cognitive inertia (the tendency of different participants to think along the same lines), production blocking (inability to produce a meaningful contribution), and domination by more knowledgeable peers (Nunamaker et al., 1991). And individuals from Far Eastern and other cultures unaccustomed to group discussions or classroom debate may be even more reluctant to participate (Ottewill and Laughton, 2000; Middleton and Rodgers, 1999).

CMCS are designed to overcome many of the factors that constrain participation in face-to-face discussions (Hiltz & Wellman, 1997). They can increase the gains from group processes such as synergy, pooling of information, objective evaluation, cognitive stimulation, and learning; and can decrease group process losses such as fragmentation, blocking, domination, evaluation apprehension, and information overload (Nunamaker et al., 1991). In particular, asynchronous interaction increases the time available to read or reread a message and formulate comments, which can improve in-depth reflection and development of a topic (Harasim, 1990). Increased opportunity for member input may also enhance the quality of decision-making (Rice, 1984).

CMCS allow everyone to participate in the discussion by providing forums that cannot be monopolized and are free of the typical factors constraining participation in a face-to-face environment. The technology has developed to the point where the quality of instructor-student interaction approaches that in the actual classroom (May, 1997). The system organizes the contributions and maintains a written transcript of the interaction that can be revised, stored and retrieved later (Harasim, 1990). Moreover, the need to verbalize all aspects of interaction by writing can enhance meta-cognitive skills such as self-reflection and revision in learning (Harasim, 1990).

The communication system provides a democratic setting. Students have more control over their own participation than in a face-to-face environment. Everyone is perceived on a similar basis regardless of nationality, accent, assertiveness in face-to-face discussions, and other characteristics that would tend to put students on unequal footing in the typical classroom setting (Johnstone, 1991). Thus students from cultures that shy away from direct criticism and face-to-face confrontation can use the CMCS to comment critically (but anonymously) on the ideas contributed by others (Lewis, 1996).

One major set of disadvantages of CMCS to support case discussions stems from the temporal dimension of the communication. For example, in computer-mediated same-time discussions participants may suffer from cognitive inertia and production blocking during the discussion. In computer-mediated asynchronous case discussions, participants may not participate at all or may experience anxiety due to delays and different participation rates (Benbunan-Fich and Hiltz, 1999; Chappell and Schermerhorn, 1999).

Other disadvantages stem from purely practical considerations, such as the need for at least minimal typing proficiency in order to get one's thoughts into written form. The participant must also have an adequate level of competence in the particular computer program or language used by the given CMCS. Some degree of spontaneity and even enthusiasm may be lost during the time required to type one's thoughts and/or format and transmit them properly. For non-native English speakers working with native English speakers on cases written in English (or for any participant working in a second language in which he or she is not completely comfortable), the necessity of composing, typing and transmitting in the non-native language may be quite daunting (Eren, 1992).

Another set of disadvantages may arise from the inability of faculty members to structure or administer CMC-based learning exercises: a survey by Mueller et al. (2001) identified inadequate training, excessive preparation time, lack of staff support, and lack of knowledge about how to implement specific software presentation packages as the major obstacles preventing more widespread use of CMCS in classrooms.

AN INTEGRATIVE FRAMEWORK

Computer-mediated communication to support case discussions can be classified in terms of the framework proposed by Johansen (1992). The framework was originally designed to describe different modes of interaction according to two dimensions: time and place. Interaction can occur at the same time (synchronous) or at different times (asynchronous). Members can meet in the same place (proximate) or in different places (different).

Figure 1 shows different alternatives for the using CMCS as the discussion medium for case study activities.

FIGURE 1. CMC-Based Discussion of Case Studies

		Time Same	Different
Place	Same	1. Decision room CMCS	3. Web-based case studies
	Different	2. Chat Rooms Desktop-video conferences	4. Asynchronous Learning Networks (ALNs) E-mail or Threaded Discussions

Adapted from Johansen (1992)

Same time/same place refers to situations in which traditional classroom discussions are conducted via computer instead of verbally. In this mode of interaction, the group meets face-to-face but exchanges information using a real-time communication system (Alavi, 1994). Housed in a "decision room," the system usually consists of networked computer workstations for participants and a facilitator, a large public screen to display the results of group discussion, and software to support group processes such as brainstorming, voting and ranking (Alavi et al., 1997).

Same time/different place situations occur when cases are discussed at the same time but the students are located in different places. The exchange of information takes place through chat rooms or video and data links across locations (Alavi et al., 1995; Webster & Hackley, 1997).

Different time/same place normally refers to the case in which people work in shifts but share a common meeting room or project room where they leave messages for each other and share materials (Johansen, 1992). A possible application to case study discussions would be a web site where the students could get case information. The case would be in the same virtual place, but the students could go there at different times.

Different time/different place refers to totally distant discussions in which team members rarely meet face-to-face. The members are dispersed across different locations and the discussion takes place asynchronously, using email or threaded discussions forums.

APPLICATION TO CROSS-NATIONAL IB CASE DISCUSSIONS

Case discussions can be carried out in any cell of the time/place framework, using synchronous or asynchronous CMCS, depending on the temporal and spatial dimensions of the communication. Groups with remote participants meeting in real-time can use chat rooms or desktop-video conferences to carry out their discussions. And groups meeting asynchronously can use e-mail or threaded discussions to support their electronic discussions.

Same time/same place discussions using a decision-room: CMCS may promote more honest comments and challenges even by participants from strongly objectivist educational traditions because of the possibility of keeping their opinions and contributions anonymous through the medium. Participation might be further enhanced by devising appropriate rules and procedures; for example, the instructor could specify time periods during which each participant was required to type his/her thoughts and ideas privately, after which all participants' files would be displayed simultaneously. Another possibility would be to invite participants to comment on, edit or modify each other's screed, again anonymously.

Same time/different place discussions in some ways could be the most ideal application of CMCS to promote cross-national interactions because this approach allows participation by teams of participants impossible to assemble in a face-to-face meeting (Hiltz, 1994). This approach could allow for real-time exchanges through chat rooms or desktop video conferences by teams in different countries whose time zones were not *too* different, for example, between countries on the same continent or on different continents but fairly similar longitudes (e.g., North and South America). It could even allow for such exchanges among countries halfway around the world from each other if the team in one country was willing to get up in the middle of the night to participate.

The mechanics of the exercise would be important. One approach would be for participant teams to discuss an assigned case among themselves (either face-to-face or using video-conferencing systems), to agree upon their best approach to handling the problems in the case, and then to compare their analysis to analyses by the instructor or other teams. The cross-cultural dimension would be achieved by having teams in different countries compare their solutions to the case, ideally supplemented with a discussion of the assumptions, the critical factors, and the desirability of different outcomes underlying each team's approach. If the case involved an investment in a given country, it would be particularly desirable if one or more teams from that country could participate so as to add their perspective to the discussion.

A second approach, more difficult to organize and coordinate but ultimately a richer cross-cultural experience, would be to form cross-national teams to work together from the beginning of the discussion.

Another variation particularly suited to CMCS-based interactions would be negotiation exercises between teams from different countries or cultures (Ruhe and Allen, 2001; May, 1997). These exercises, which may be based on relatively short, simple cases or lengthy, complex ones, usually concern either the terms of entry for a multinational investor from one country into a foreign country or a dispute that has arisen between parties from different countries. A team from one culture could of course play one role, while a team from another culture assumed the role of another party.

Because the discussions would be carried on in real time in cells 1 and 2, a high degree of spontaneity and brainstorming-type interactions in the technology-mediated discussions should be possible.

Different time/same place discussions could have various applications for cross-cultural case analyses. If the instructor used the same case in more than one class, he/she could set up a sort of dialog between the classes, with each class in turn reviewing the previous class's comments and adding their own further thoughts. Day (full-time) and evening (frequently part-time) classes might bring quite different perspectives to a given case, for example. It might even be desirable to have classes in different subjects–for instance, a class in international economics and one in international relations–analyze a case that had both economic and political dimensions (as is true of many international trade issues, for example). Or again, if one class had a predominance of students from an objectivist learning tradition and another from predominantly constructivist backgrounds, use of CMCS could help break down the barriers and encourage more open communication between them.

An interesting application in this cell is the use of web-based case studies. Students can explore a hypermedia environment to gather case information. The case would be located in the "same virtual place," but teams could go there at different times. For an example of this new generation of interactive web-based case studies, visit <http://www.theKendalls.org>.

Different time/different place discussions could well be the most common type of cross-cultural interaction using CMCS for teaching and learning of IB cases, involving, of course, individuals or teams from widely-separated parts of the world.

One of the challenges for designers of CMCS is to provide effective coordination tools (such as agenda, voting, and polling) for structuring asynchronous interactions so as to overcome the inherent limitations of the medium (Dufner et al., 1994). This is particularly important when team members are dispersed across locations and in different time zones.

One situation in which these problems may be less serious, however, is negotiation exercises based on complex scenarios such as the Harvard Business School type of cases where spontaneous, brainstorming-type interactions are not really desirable. Rather, each participant team would need time to consider the other's proposals, so the asynchronous nature of cell-4 interactions would actually be an advantage. Furthermore, the distinction between objectivist and constructivist approaches would be less of a barrier in this type of negotiation because the interactions are somewhat more adversarial, especially at the beginning of the negotiation. Indeed, it is even possible that the use of CMCS would facilitate the process of gradually narrowing differences and reaching consensus.

OBSERVATIONS AND CONCLUSIONS

New computer-mediated communication alternatives offer a wide range of possibilities to improve case discussion by removing the time and place barriers associated with traditional in-class exchanges. In the context of International Business courses, these new communication tools can also be used to include multi-cultural perspectives by bringing people from other countries and locations into the case discussions. The framework presented in this paper offers a guide to designing and implementing such innovations in case discussions in IB courses.

The framework can also guide research efforts aimed at discovering and documenting the actual learning gains achieved by these new methods or at comparing the effectiveness of the different alternatives under similar situations. This type of research is already under way in other disciplines such as Information Systems and Management, but it is not as far advanced in IB education, understandably so in view of the greater complexity of implementation across national boundaries, diverse cultures and large distances. The framework can guide efforts to bring the field of IB up to the level of sophistication of those other disciplines.

At an operational level, CMCS can promote more interactive learning for participants from objectivist traditions by removing or at least reducing feelings of awkwardness, reluctance to challenge authority figures such as course instructors, and cultural inhibitions against disagreeing with colleagues or acquaintances. They can also enhance performance of cross-cultural and cross-national groups, due in part to the visibility that the system can provide to each response, combined with deeper reflection in asynchronous work. Thus they can aid in narrowing of the gap between objectivist and constructivist approaches to case learning.

There can also be a reverse benefit, however: participants schooled in constructivist approaches may gain more understanding of the thinking and behaviors of participants from objectivist backgrounds and may thus improve their own abilities to interact and reach agreement with their opposite numbers. Thus Western-educated participants may come to appreciate the unique perspectives and contributions that persons from non-Western educational traditions can offer.

NOTE

1. Stake (1994) proposed a similar dichotomy in learning from case studies: teaching didactically involves conveying what the instructor has learned from the case, whereas in discovery learning the instructor provides material and invites participants to identify and discuss issues on among themselves. See also Bates (1990).

REFERENCES

Alavi, M. (1994). Computer-mediated collaborative learning: An empirical evaluation. *MIS Quarterly*. June, 150-174.

Alavi, M., Wheeler, B., & Valacich, J. (1995). Using IT to reengineer business education: An exploratory investigation to collaborative telelearning. *MIS Quarterly*, September, 294-312.

Alavi, M., Yoo, Y., & Vogel, D. (1997). Using Information Technology to add value to management education. *Academy of Management Journal*, 40 (6), 1310-1333.

Althaus, S.L. (1997). Computer-mediated communication in the university classroom: An experiment with on-line discussion. *Communication Education*, July, 158-174.

Barnes, L., Christensen, R., & Hansen, A. (1994). *Teaching and the case method*. Boston, MA: Harvard Business School Press.

Bates, A.W. (1990). Interactivity as a Criterion for Media Selection in Distance Education. Washington, D.C.: U.S. Government Printing Office. (ERIC Document Reproduction Service, No. ED 329 245).

Benbunan-Fich, R. (1997). *Effects of computer-mediated communication systems on learning, performance and satisfaction: A comparison of groups and individuals solving ethical scenarios*. Ph.D. Dissertation, Rutgers University, Newark, NJ. UMI Dissertation Services # 9729583.

Benbunan-Fich, R. (1998). Guidelines for using case scenarios to teach computer ethics. *ACM SIGCAS*, September, 20-24.

Benbunan-Fich, R. and Hiltz, S.R. 1999. "Educational Applications of CMCS: Solving Case Studies through Asynchronous Learning Networks." *Journal of Computer-Mediated Communication*, 4(3), March. <http://www.ascusc.org/jcmc/vol4/issue3/benbunan-fich.html>.

Bouton, C. and Garth, R.Y. (1983). *Learning in Groups* . San Francisco: Jossey-Bass, Inc.

Chappell, David S., and John R. Schermerhorn, Jr. (1999) Introducing International Business Experience through Virtual Teamwork. *Journal of Teaching in International Business* 10(3/4), 43-59.

Chizmar, J., & Williams, D. (1996). Altering time and space through network technologies to enhance learning. *Cause/Effect*, 19 (3), 14-21.

Dufner, D., Hiltz, R., & Turoff, M. (1994). Distributed Group Support: A preliminary analysis of the effects of the use of voting tools and sequential procedures. *HICSS Proceedings.*

Eren, Saban (1992). Computer Aided Education: Issues and Strategies–A Case Study of Turkey. *Journal of Teaching in International Business*, Vol.3, no. 4, 45-57.

Fjermestad, J., Hiltz, S. R., & Turoff, M. (1993). An integrated framework for the study of group decision support systems. *HICSS Proceedings*, Vol. IV, 179-188.

Galegher, J., & Kraut, R.R. (1994). Computer-mediated communication for intellectual teamwork: An experiment in group writing. *Information Systems Research*, 5(2), 110-138.

Harasim, L., Hiltz, S.R., Teles, L., & Turoff, M. (1995). *Learning networks: A field guide to teaching and learning online*. Cambridge, MA: MIT Press.

Harasim, L. Ed. (1990). *On-line education: Perspectives on a new medium*. New York: Praeger/Greenwood.

Hashim, S., Rathnam, S. & Whiston, A. (1991). CATT: An argumentation based groupware system for enhancing case discussion in business schools. *Proceedings of the International Conference on Information Systems (ICIS)*, 371-385.

Hiltz, S.R. (1994). *The Virtual Classroom: Learning without limits via computer networks*. Norwood, New Jersey: Ablex Publishing Corporation.

Hiltz, S.R. and Turoff, M. 1993. *The Network Nation: Human Communication via Computer*, Revised Edition, MIT Press.

Hiltz, S. R., & Wellman, B. (1997). Asynchronous learning networks as a virtual classroom. *Communications of the ACM*, 40 (9), September, 44-49.

Johansen, R. (1992). An introduction to computer augmented teamwork. In Bostrom, Watson, & Kinney, Eds. *Computer augmented teamwork: A guided tour*. New York: Van Nostrand Reinhold.

Johnson, D.W. (1981). "Student-student Interaction: The Neglected Variable in Education." *Educational Research*, Vol.10, N.1, 5-10.

Johnstone, S. (1991). "Research on Telecommunicated Learning: Past, Present and Future." *The Annals of the American Academy of Political and Social Science*, Vol. 514, March, 49-57.

Kendall, J.E., Kendall, K.E., Baskerville, R. and Barnes, R. 1996. "An Empirical Comparison of a Hypertext based systems Analysis Case with Conventional Cases and Role Playing." *The Data Base for Advances in Information Systems*, winter, Vol. 27, N. 1, 58-77. HyperCase can be found on the Web, <http://www.thekendalls.org>.

Klass, Desmond, and Alma M. Whiteley (1996). Combining Strategic Technologies to Facilitate the Teaching of International Business. *Journal of Teaching in International Business*, Vol. 7, no. 4, 49-64.

LaRose, R., Gregg, J., & Eastin, M. (1998). Audiographic telecourses for the Web: An experiment. *Journal of Computer-Mediated Communication* [On-line], 4 (2). Available: <http://www.ascusc.org/jcmc/vol4/issue2/larose.html>.

Leidner, D., & Jarvenpaa, S. (1995). The use of Information Technology to enhance management school education: A theoretical view. *MIS Quarterly*. September, 265-291.

Leidner, D., & Fuller, M. (1996). Improving student processing and assimilation of conceptual information: GSS-supported collaborative learning vs. individual constructive learning. *Proceedings of HICSS 29th*. January, 293-302.

Lewis, L. Floyd (1996). Using Group Support Systems (GSS) in the Teaching of International Business. *Journal of Teaching in International Business*, Vol. 7, no. 4, 31-47.

May, Bruce E. (1997) Curriculum Internationalization and Distance Learning: Convergence of Necessity and Technology. *Journal of Teaching in International Business*, Vol. 9, no. 1, 35-50.

Middleton, Karen L., and Jacci L. Rodgers (1999). Communication Across Cultures: Classroom Dilemmas from a Global Perspective. *Journal of Teaching in International Business*, Vol. 11, no. 2, 21-37.

Mueller, Carolyn B., Gordon Jones, David A. Ricks, Bodo B. Schlegelmilch, and Cheryl A. Van Deusen (2001). Information and Communication Technology in the Classroom: An Empirical Study with an International Perspective. *Journal of Teaching in International Business*, 12(3), 21-41.

Nunamaker, J., Dennis, A., Valacich, J., Vogel, D., & George, J. (1991). Electronic meeting systems to support group work. *Communications of the ACM*, 34 (7), 41-61.

Ocker, R., Hiltz, S. R., Turoff, M., & Fjermestad, J. (1995). The effects of distributed group support and process structuring on software requirements development teams: Results on creativity and quality. *Journal of Management Information Systems*, 12, 3, Winter.

Ottewill, Roger, and David Laughton (2000). East Meets West: Using Multi-Cultural Groupwork to Develop the Cross-Cultural Capability of Tomorrow's International Managers. *Journal of Teaching in International Business*, Vol. 12, no. 1, 1-22.

Parhizgar, Kamal Dean (1998). International Cross-Cultural Collaborative Teaching and Training Theories (ICCCTTT). *Journal of Teaching in International Business* 9(3), 21-41.

Pedhazur, E., & Pedhazur, L. (1991). *Measurement, design and analysis: An integrated approach*. Lawrence Earlbaum Associates, Publishers.

Peek, L.E., Peek, G.S. & Horras, M. (1994). Enhancing Arthur Andersen business ethics vignettes: Group discussions using cooperative/collaborative learning techniques. *Journal of Business Ethics*. Vol, 13, 189-196.

Perrone, C., Repenning, A., Spencer, S., & Ambach, J. (1996). Computers in the classroom: Moving from tool to medium. *Journal of Computer-Mediated Communication* [On-line], 2(3) <http://www.ascusc.org/jcmc/vol2/issue3/perrone.html>.

Pinsonneault, A., & Kraemer, K.L. (1989). The Impact of technological support on groups: An assessment of the empirical research. *Decision Support Systems*, 5, 197-216.

Pisani, Michael J. (2000). An American Management Training Model in a Latin American Context Some Implications for International Business Consultants. *Journal of Teaching in International Business*, Vol. 12, no. 1, 23-39.

Rice, R. (1984). *The new media: Communication, research & technology*. Beverly Hills: Sage.

Ruhe, John A., and William R. Allen (2001). NEWS Ltd.: Simulations for Trust Development. *Journal of Teaching in International Business*, Vol. 12, no. 4, 29-47.

Salomon, G., & Globerson, T. (1989). When teams do not function the way the ought to. *Journal of Educational Research*, 13 (1), 89-100.

Scott, Don, Catherine Durnell Cramton, Stephane Gauvin, Beata Lobert Jones, and Gerhard Steinke (1999). Crossing the International Teaching Divide–The Evaluation of an Internet Based Teaching Project. *Journal of Teaching in International Business*, Vol. 10, no. 3/4, 61-79.

Shepperd, J.A. (1993). Productivity loss in performance groups: A motivation analysis. *Psychological Bulletin*, 113 (1), 67-81.

Shuell, T. 1986. "Cognitive Conceptions of Learning." *Review of Educational Research, Winter*, Vol. 56, N. 4, 411-436.

Silver, M., Markus, L., & Beath, C. (1995). The Information Technology interaction model: A foundation for the MBA core course. *MIS Quarterly*, 361-390.

Smith, David E. (1997) Distance Learning Technology for Enhancing Pedagogy: The Global Connection. *Journal of Teaching in International Business*, Vol. 8, no. 3, 1-19.

Smith, J., & Vanecek, M. (1988). Computer conferencing and task-oriented decision: implications for group decision support. *Information and Management*, 14, 123-132.

Stake, R.E. (1994) Case Studies. In Denzin, N., and Y. Lincoln, eds., *Handbook of Qualitative Research*. London: Sage.

Taggert, J., C. Wheeler and S. Young (1994). The Training of International Managers: The Strathclyde Perspective. *Journal of Teaching in International Business*, Vol. 6, no. 2: 1-21.

Webster, J., & Hackley, P. (1997). Teaching effectiveness in technology-mediated distance learning. *Academy of Management Journal*, 40 (6), 1282-1309.

Wheeler, B.C., Valacich, J.S., Alavi, M., & Vogel, D. (1995). A framework for technology-mediated inter-institutional telelearning relationships. *Journal of Computer-Mediated Communication* [On-line], 1 (1). Available: <http://www.ascusc.org/jcmc/vol1/issue1/wheeler/essay.html>.

Whitely, Alma M. (1996). The Hegemony of Western Business Management Literature in Non-Western Settings: A Hong Kong Study. *Journal of Teaching in International Business*, Vol. 7, no. 4, 65-89.

Wilson, E.V., Morrison, J.P., & Napier, A.M (1997). Perceived effectiveness of computer-mediated communications and face-to-face communications in student software development teams. *Journal of Computer Information Systems*, Winter, 2-7.

Digital Technology in Teaching International Business: Is a Tradeoff Between Richness and Reach Required?

Cliff Wymbs
Hugo Kijne

SUMMARY. As we enter the brave new world of interactive digital technology, teachers of International Business are being confronted with the problems and opportunities associated with integrating the new medium with a subject area that is inherently geographically dispersed. This analysis extends the traditional marketing tradeoffs between richness (depth of knowledge) and reach (geographic area coverage) to the emerging technology-mediated education industry, and then specifically evaluates their effect on the teaching of International Business. We believe that interactive learning, particularly as it applies to team building and problem solving in a multicultural environment, will prove valuable as the next generation of business leaders begins to emerge from academic institutions. *[Article copies available for a fee from The Haworth Document Delivery Service: 1-800-HAWORTH. E-mail address: <getinfo@*

Cliff Wymbs is affiliated with the Zicklin School of Business, Baruch College/CUNY, Marketing Department, B12-240, One Bernard Baruch Way, New York, NY 10010 (E-mail: Clifford_Wymbs@baruch.cuny.edu). Hugo Kijne is affiliated with the College of Staten Island/CUNY, 2800 Victory Boulevard, Staten Island, NY 10314 (E-mail: kijne@postbox.csi.cuny.edu).

[Haworth co-indexing entry note]: "Digital Technology in Teaching International Business: Is a Tradeoff Between Richness and Reach Required?" Wymbs, Cliff, and Hugo Kijne. Co-published simultaneously in *Journal of Teaching in International Business* (International Business Press, an imprint of The Haworth Press, Inc.) Vol. 14, No. 2/3, 2003, pp. 29-40; and: *Digital Technology in Teaching International Business* (ed: Lloyd C. Russow) International Business Press, an imprint of The Haworth Press, Inc., 2003, pp. 29-40. Single or multiple copies of this article are available for a fee from The Haworth Document Delivery Service [1-800-HAWORTH 9:00 a.m. - 5:00 p.m. (EST). E-mail address: getinfo@haworthpress.com].

KEYWORDS. International business, richness and reach, culture, teaching

INTRODUCTION

Education in general and the teaching of International Business in particular are exploring technology extensions to enhance student learning.[1] Teachers and business people alike want prospective employees to be better trained to be able to function more efficiently in the international business environment. The use of the Internet has the potential to greatly affect the reach of teaching International Business (courses can be taught across continents) and dramatically improve the richness (students can be exposed to cross-cultural negotiations and problem solving). The unique aspects of international business, i.e., sensitivity to culture, exposure to diverse political regimes, complex behavioral interactions, make it an ideal candidate for technological experimentation by the academic community. We discuss how students can use the Internet as a medium to personally participate in international problem solving exercises. Students who use this approach to gain a good appreciation of foreign cognitive, affective and behavioral patterns will be in a better position to become future international business leaders. The challenge is how to use technology to accomplish this goal.

As we enter the brave new world of interactive digital technology, traditional teaching methods are being criticized as passive knowledge delivery processes with much need for improvement (Ueltschy, 2001). These include:

- *Sage-on-the-stage*–the traditional instructor-centered classroom approach, where one instructor services between twenty and thirty students.
- *Sage-on-screen*–the same as sage-on-stage, only now the sage is multiplied by a real time broadcast to distant locations. Experience teaches that two distant locations are the most the sage can handle.
- *Sage-on-paper* or traditional distance learning–correspondence courses with incidental telephone contact between a faculty member (or a tutor) and the student.

However, equally unsatisfactory are initial online approaches that beam courses to students and treat them as objects rather than active subjects, i.e., the pump and dump approach (Hanley, 2001).

Egemen, Edwards, and Nirmalakhandan (1998) assert that one of the main prerequisites for improving the teaching-learning process is active and interactive participation of students. Fitzgerald (1995) highlights the important role interactive technologies can play in bridging the gap between knowledge acquisition, skill development and real-world application. Emerging methods include:

- *Web-based-sage-on-the-stage* or sage-on-screen–supported by a website with posted lecture notes, a syllabus, an outline and other course materials.
- *Sage-on-the-Web*–an instructor-centered course delivered via the Internet. Lecture notes, a syllabus, an outline and other course materials have been posted on a website or are posted on a weekly basis. Threaded discussions (e-conferences) are the main tool of communication between the instructor and the students.
- *Internet-distance-learning*–has elements of traditional distance learning (sage-on-paper) combined with the Internet and a variety of feedback loops between instructor and students. This approach will be discussed in detail later in the article.
- *Pure-on-line* education–where all course materials, such as syllabus, outline, lecture notes, textbook, video, and audio are only available in electronic format, via the course website, and all interactivity and feedback is pre-programmed and automatic.

Teachers of International Business are well aware of the problems and opportunities associated with teaching subject matter that is geographically remote. Over the years, a limited number of expensive programs have been developed to give students rich individual experiences associated with foreign travel. However, only recently has Internet technology been used to increase the availability and reduce the cost of interactive programs connecting students from geographically dispersed locations (Pettijohn, 2000). This analysis extends the traditional marketing tradeoffs between richness (depth of knowledge) and reach (geographic area coverage) to the emerging technology-mediated education industry, and then specifically evaluates their effect on the teaching of International Business (Evans & Wurster, 1997). However, before we begin the analysis, it is instructive to provide a common understanding of the dynamics associated with the teaching of the somewhat unique field of International Business (IB).

INTERNATIONAL BUSINESS PEDAGOGICAL PROBLEMS

International Business, by its very nature, deals with more than one country. One of the key objectives of any instructor who teaches a course in IB is to get students to remove their home country blinders and begin to appreciate the political, social, cultural and economic nuances associated with doing business in a foreign country. Unlike functional business majors who see every day their discipline being applied around them, IB students must partially rely on other people's accounts to appreciate the nuances of the field. Lectures, cases studies and instructors' relating their international experiences have been the traditional ways to convey this information (Pettijohn, 2000). Teaching students that norms, values and beliefs of workers and managers in one part of the world are different than those of people in another is a necessary first step; however, any IB executive will tell you that experiential learning which involves cognitive, affective and behavioral contact with foreigners is the best way to accumulate the tacit knowledge necessary to successfully conduct international business. Unfortunately, traditional teaching methods of IB do not provide students with a true appreciation of what it takes to do business in foreign countries.

One solution put forth in many executive MBA programs is to bring students to the foreign workplace via a one to two-week trip to a foreign country (Decker, 1999). As mentioned before, another limited approach, used more at the undergraduate level, is for students to spend one or two semesters abroad learning about language and culture. Each approach has it merits, but neither truly simulates a real world business situation and both are very expensive.[2] We as educators are left with the question of how can we cost effectively train students to become effective in dealing with the exploding number of international business opportunities?

RICHNESS AND REACH APPROACH

Evans and Wurster (1997) state that the Internet is causing a fundamental shift in the economics of information–a shift that will precipitate changes in the structure of entire industries. We feel that, with minor adaptation, their thesis can be applied to the education industry in general and the teaching of International Business specifically. The basic tenets of the thesis are:

> To the extent information is embedded in the physical mode of delivery, its economics is governed by a basic law: the trade-off between richness and reach. Reach simply means the number of people, at home or at work, exchanging information. Richness is defined by three aspects of the information itself. The first is bandwidth, or the amount of information that can be moved from sender to receiver in a given time . . . The second aspect is the degree to which the information is customized . . . The third aspect is interactivity. Dialogue is possible for a small group, but to reach millions of people the message must be a monologue.
>
> In general, the communication of rich information has required proximity and dedicated channels whose costs or physical constraints have limited the size of the audience to which the information can be sent. Conversely, the communication of information to a large audience required compromises in bandwidth, customization, and interactivity . . .
>
> The tradeoff between richness and reach . . . not only governs the old economics of information but also is fundamental to a whole set of premises about how the business world works. And it is precisely this trade-off that is being blown apart. (Evans & Wurster, 1997, 4, 5)

In effect, the Internet permits a company to have here-to-fore unheard of opportunities of wide reach (size of audience), great richness (customized products) and strong affiliation (personalized responses to customers interests) (Dunning & Wymbs, 2001). We believe the education industry over time will be one of the businesses that will experience fundamental change along the richness, reach and customization dimensions. Limiting penetration are the need for social interaction, institutional constraints and general bureaucratic impediments associated with teacher unions, tenure and inertia. However, technology, private enterprise, and instructor creativity are creating a variety of market solutions that are beginning to complement traditional educational approaches.

APPLICATION OF TECHNOLOGY TO EDUCATION– NEW APPROACHES EMERGING

Defeating geographic barriers in education is not new, it has been accomplished via correspondence courses using mail, telephones and faxes for decades. However, only in the last five years has the emergence of advanced communication technologies dramatically enhanced the number of new opportunities for collaboration among educational institutions. As technology creates new possibilities, administrators, students and especially faculty must carefully question the value payoff of these new educational forms, yet, they must also be willing to reassess long-held assumptions of the current educational paradigm (Wheeler, Valacich, Alavi, Vogel, 2001). We now explore in detail the newly emerging "Internet-distance-learning" approach. Then we will compare the traditional classroom approach and six technology-enabled teaching modalities along the richness and reach dimensions outlined earlier.

Before we compare these six modalities, however, we briefly describe the Internet-distance-learning approach as provided by the United States Open University. It starts with the instructor-of-record defining the learning outcomes which students are expected to acquire through their study of the course. He/she supervises the course delivery by the Associated Faculty and is ultimately responsible for the quality of course delivery and grading equity. Courses are deliberately designed to achieve these learning outcomes through the provision of multiple-media learning materials and personalized teaching, learning feedback and support from Associate Faculty. The learning materials may take the form of high quality printed course texts, video and audio recordings, software and interactive CD-ROMs. A specially developed website is integral to each course. Each student is assigned to a member of the Associate Faculty who provides individual support in a variety of ways: computer mediated, including e-mail and asynchronous conferencing, telephone, or written. The combination of high quality materials coupled with outstanding study support provides students with rich and varied learning opportunities (USOU, 2000).

In this concept, two traditional classroom roles of an instructor–introducing students to new content (the *teacher* role), and facilitating learning by answering questions, moderating discussions and tutoring students individually (the *enabler* role)–are divided between the Study Guide and the Associate Faculty. The Study Guide, written course material, introduces the students to content and guides them through the substance of their learning journey, and the Associate Faculty facilitates, responds to questions, moderates, tutors, in short, enables. E-tivities,[3] e-conferencing and individual e-mail are the only exchanges between Associated Faculty and students. Since one Associated Faculty usually services only one section of a course, and course materials are highly standardized, reach is unlimited as long as on-line services function properly, while richness depends on the quality of the study guide/textbook/other course materials/e-tivities mix.

RICHNESS AND REACH COMPARISONS

1. Sage-on-stage: Richness is contingent upon the qualities of the sage, with regard to content and with regard to presentation, as well as upon student numbers (classes with 200 students hardly allow for robust two-way communication, which reduces richness; very small classes, seminars or tutorials may be richer than a class with a regular size).
2. Sage-on-screen: Reach obviously increases, but richness may decrease somewhat, since the need to switch back and forth between three locations during Q&A sessions and classroom discussions significantly reduces classroom spontaneity.
3. Sage-on-paper or traditional distance learning: Reach is unlimited as long as the postal and telephone services function properly, richness is limited by the medium and the lack of interactivity and immediate feedback. This approach was used by Athabasca University in Canada and by the Dutch Open University, but both are now moving toward Internet-distance learning.
4. Web-based-sage-on-the-stage: Does not increase the reach beyond the number of students, but may increase richness depending on the availability of the instructor elsewhere and the quality of the posted material.
5. Sage-on-the-Web: Richness depends on the quality of the sage and posted materials, reach on the number of sections an instructor can handle (2 or 3 at most).
6. Internet-distance-learning: In spite of the unlimited reach, the Associated Faculty formula allows for a dialogue rather than a monologue, at least in the sections of the course where learning is facilitated, and thus one of Evans and Wurster's (1997) proclaimed limitations of high richness programs is partly overcome.

7. Pure-on-line education: Reach may be higher than in the Internet-distance learning approach because Internet access is the only requirement for participation in the course, although quality delivery of streaming video may require bandwidth to which not all students have access, thereby limiting reach. New instructional tools such as Prentice Hall's ActiveBooks will enhance the development of this approach.

APPROACHES THAT BEST FIT THE INTERNATIONAL BUSINESS ENVIRONMENT

The introduction of e-learning has greatly expanded the number of educational alternatives to instructors and students alike. We now specifically address the effectiveness of these educational approaches in the space of international business along the dimensions of richness and reach. It appears that sage-on-the-Web and Internet-distance-learning expand the reach associated with the number of students that can be simultaneously taught IB and improve the richness associated with the teaching of individual students. Both sage-on-the-Web and Internet-distance learning can bring together students from different parts of the world via the Internet through threaded discussions. At a minimum, the classroom reach can be extended by having students electronically discuss culturally diverse perspectives of IB problems, but a much richer exchange is possible if students from different countries work in teams to simultaneously solve international business problems.[4] The very basic constraints associated with the traditional teaching methods of IB, distance and time, can be used by students to enhance the learning experience.

However, the teaching of IB in an international environment through electronic medium is not free of problems. There is a tremendous administrative burden that must be overcome. Coordination cost associated with curriculum development among geographically diverse educational institutions is substantial. Technology interfaces can also be troublesome. Even easy to understand items such as revenue sharing can be quite difficult to decide, while difficult areas such as intellectual property ownership can be nightmarish. International marketing efforts alone cannot guarantee that an "ideal" cultural mix of students can be registered for IB courses, and even when such an ideal mix can be brought together, a culturally diverse group of students completing complex assignments will probably go through a similar extension of the formative stages of group dynamics that culturally diverse groups, which are physically located together and working in real time, go through (Watson, Kumar and Michaelsen, 1993).

IMPACT OF CULTURE ON THE IB EDUCATION PROCESS

Beaton (2001) states that if the U.S. is to continue to maintain its competitive advantage in the global marketplace, educational institutions must prepare the next generation of business leaders for a pluralistic world in which multiculturalism dominates and international business education is multidimensional. As part of this education process, Scott (1996) asserts that effective international business communication skills are the backbone that supports the transaction of business around the world. He believes that the goal of international business communication instruction in the 21st century should be the development of cultural fluency, the ability to cross cultural boundaries and function like a native (Scott, 1999). The findings of Ueltschy (2001) confirm those of Roach, Johnston and Hair (1993), i.e., the integration of interactive technology in the curriculum is beneficial in terms of increased student participation, improved team-building skills, while the Hilton and Kameda (1999) study went further and demonstrated via a case study of U.S. and Japanese students that the Internet and e-mail can be used as an efficient and effective international communication teaching device.

In addition to the above benefits, there are also cultural impediments associated with teaching and learning in a computer mediated IB environment. Historically, French students expect the professor to answer all questions; Japanese students rarely question the professor and American students are more interactive (Adler 1997). What happens when each is exposed to the other in cyberspace? The good news is that this problem solving by doing in the university environment will likely lessen problems in the business world. In fact, Hilton and Kamaeda (1999) observed that communicating electronically across cultures can help encourage candor and assist in accommodating language differences. Most students studying in another country are more proficient at reading than they are in talking in a foreign language. This is because reading does not require real time processing while talking does. When reading, a student is free to look up words and ask others about meaning. Written material from an instructor usually has much less jargon, fewer cultural analogies and is more direct and to the point.

CONCLUSION

Education in general, and the teaching of International Business in particular, is rapidly adopting technology to enhance student learning. Teachers and business people alike want prospective employees to be better trained to be able to function more efficiently in the international business environment. The use of the Internet has the potential to affect greatly the reach[5] of teaching International Business (courses can be taught across continents to business people who have access to the Internet but no time for traditional education) and to improve dramatically the richness of the course (students can be exposed to cross-cultural negotiations and problem solving). The unique aspects of international business, i.e., the need to discuss problems that affect persons in more than one nation, make it an ideal candidate for experimentation by the academic community. We have discussed how students can use Internet technology to personally participate in international problem solving exercises, particularly via sage-on-the-Web and Internet-distance-learning approaches. We believe that this learning by doing approach, particularly as it applies to team building and problem solving in a multicultural environment, will prove valuable as the next generation of business leaders begins to emerge from academic institutions. We also believe that considerable experimentation will continue to take place as Internet technology evolves and best practices begin to be established in the teaching of International Business.

FUTURE RESEARCH

This article defined the various approaches being used to teach international business and provided subjective evaluations of each along richness and reach dimensions. A logical next step is to do survey research and test how students and faculty evaluate each alternative along consistent learning objectives and preferences and to specifically evaluate the richness and reach attributes.

NOTES

1. Dozens of traditional universities and colleges have joined new for-profit start-ups like University of Phoenix to mine the Web student revenue dollars. Venture capital investment in education has climbed from $500M in 1997 to $2.5 billion in 2000 (Hanley, 2001). On-line competition and technological advances in communica-

tions have caused many traditional universities to experiment with new educational approaches.

2. Many international business opportunities involve groups of people from multiple countries that come together for a reasonably short period of time to solve a particular business problem. The meteoric increase in the number of international alliances, joint ventures and acquisitions over the past decade provides strong support for the above assertion (Dunning, 1996; Gomes-Casseres, 1996).

3. Gilly Salmon, MBA Program Director of the USOU, recently coined the term "e-tivities" to bring together the practical aspects of mobilizing, engaging and effectively e-moderating in technology mediated teaching and learning environments. Her suggestion is that e-moderators create e-tivities with attention to content, process and outcomes. For references see: <http://pcbs042.open.ac.uk/gilly/>.

4. Face-to-face interactions remain the richest way to solve business problems; however, people-to-people Internet exchanges are becoming the most used form of business communication. Therefore, student experience in successfully conversing via this medium is becoming increasingly important.

5. Also reach associated with the amount of quality interaction among international students is greatly expanded. Previously to get this person-to-person international experience, travel was involved. Now all that is required is a computer terminal and a computer designed international business course.

BIBLIOGRAPHY

Adler, N. (1997). *International Dimensions of Organizational Behavior*. South-Western College Publishing. Cincinnati, OH.

Beaton, S. (2001). "The Federal role in international business education," *Thunderbird International Business Review*. 43 (2), 289-302.

Creed, T (1996). "Extending the Classroom Walls Electronically." In William Campbell and Karl Smith eds. *New Paradigms for College Teaching*, Interaction Book Co., Edina, MN.

Decker, D. (1999). "M.B.A. classes casting their aspiration abroad," *The New York Times*. November 7, 3, 12.

Dunning, J. H., (1996). "Reappraising the eclectic paradigm in an age of alliance capitalism," *Journal of International Business Studies*. V 26, 461-91.

Dunning, J. H. & Wymbs, C. (2001). "The challenge of electronic markets for international business theory," *Journal of European Business Management*. Forthcoming.

Egemen, E., Edwards, F., Nirmalakhandan, N. (1998). "Computer simulation models in environmental engineering education," *Water and Science Technology*. V 38, 295-302.

Evans, P. and Wurster, T. (1997, September-October). "Strategy and the new economics of information," *Harvard Business Review*.

Fitzgerald, O. (1995). "The effects of interactive videodisc training programs in classroom observation skills used as a teaching tool and as a learning tool," *Computers in Human Behavior*. V 11, 467-79.

Gomes-Casseres, B. (1996). *The Alliance Revolution*. Harvard University Press, Cambridge, MA.

Hanley, L. (2001, September). For-profit Internet colleges shrink–but MIT wants to be free. *Clarion*. 9.

Hilton, C. & Kameda, N. (1999). "E-mail and the Internet as international business communication teaching and research tools–a case study," *Journal of Education for Business*. V 74 (3), 181-185.

Pettijohn, J. (2000). "Virtual tools–A tool for enhancing and enlivening the international business class," *Journal of Education For Business*. V 75 (5), 291-296.

Scott. J. (1999). "Developing cultural fluency: The goal of international business communication instruction in the 21st century," *Journal of Education of Business*. V 72 (3), 140-143.

Scott, J. (1996). *Facilitating International Business Communication. A Global Perspective*. Little Rock, AR: Delta Pi Epsilon.

Ueltschy, L. (2001). "An exploratory study of integrating interactive technology into the marketing curriculum," *Journal of Marketing Education*, V 23 (1), 63-72.

USOU (2000). "United States Open University," *Undergraduate Catalog 2000-2001*, 5, 6.

Watson, Kumar and Michaelsen. (1993). "Cultural diversity's impact on interaction process and performance: Comparing homogeneous and diverse task groups," *Academy of Management Journal*, 36, 590-602.

Wheller, B., Valacich, J. Alavi, M., Vogel, D. (2001). "A framework for technology-mediated inter-institutional telelearning relationships," <http://www.ascusc.org/jcmc/vol1/issue1/wheeler/essay.htm>.

Transforming Educational and Business Practices in Belarus: Collaborative Learning at a Distance

Gaytha A. Langlois
Judy Barrett Litoff
Joseph A. Ilacqua

SUMMARY. The Bryant College Collaborative Learning at a Distance (CLD) Program in Belarus was designed to promote collaboration across diverse cultural, political, and philosophical boundaries. CLD programs can assist the Newly Independent States (NIS) in meeting the political, social, and economic challenges associated with the transition from a centralized, administrative command economy to a more democratic and diversified society. Cost-effective, collaborative distance learning projects can help to address the problem of limited educational resources and prepare faculty, undergraduates, entrepreneurs, and NGO leaders for better understanding the role of civic responsibility as a foundation for western business practices.

The ongoing Internet-based, Bryant College CLD Program, including educational institutions, research facilities and business firms, focuses

---

Gaytha A. Langlois is Professor of Environmental Policy, Judy Barrett Litoff is Professor of History, and Joseph A. Ilacqua is Professor of Economics, all at Bryant College, 1150 Douglas Pike, Smithfield, RI 02917.

This program has received funding from grants and contracts from the U.S. Departments of State, Defense, and Energy, the Higher Education Support Program (HESP) of the Open Society Institute, the John H. Chafee Center for International Business, and the Office of the Vice President for Academic Affairs, Bryant College.

[Haworth co-indexing entry note]: "Transforming Educational and Business Practices in Belarus: Collaborative Learning at a Distance." Langlois, Gaytha A., Judy Barrett Litoff, and Joseph A. Ilacqua. Co-published simultaneously in *Journal of Teaching in International Business* (International Business Press, an imprint of The Haworth Press, Inc.) Vol. 14, No. 2/3, 2003, pp. 41-66; and: *Digital Technology in Teaching International Business* (ed: Lloyd C. Russow) International Business Press, an imprint of The Haworth Press, Inc., 2003, pp. 41-66. Single or multiple copies of this article are available for a fee from The Haworth Document Delivery Service [1-800-HAWORTH 9:00 a.m. - 5:00 p.m. (EST). E-mail address: getinfo@haworthpress.com].

on a non-hierarchical model, emphasizing reciprocal, interactive learning and problem-solving. Components include Web-based courses, International Virtual Roundtable Discussions via E-mail, seminars on business skills and Web design, Internet protocol video conferencing between the U.S. and Belarus, a faculty exchange and training project, and a business internship program aimed at providing hands-on experience with business and NGO leaders in the U.S. This project demonstrates that Internet-based, collaborative learning can transcend cultural and language barriers and advance the development of a business environment supportive to the entrepreneurial spirit.

KEYWORDS. Distance learning, Belarus, Newly Independent States (NIS), Web projects, International Virtual Roundtable Discussions (IVRD), collaborative learning, Community Connections Business Program, Center for International Collaboration

INTRODUCTION

The collapse of the Soviet Union has brought enormous economic consequences to Belarus and the other Newly Independent States (NIS), and has resulted in change in all segments of these transitional societies. Creation of a stable economy, marked by a business environment favoring the entrepreneurial spirit, has been remarkably elusive. Belarusian entrepreneurs face considerable obstacles when initiating new business ventures or attempting to privatize and restructure Soviet-style production centers. They often encounter repressive business regulations, unequal taxing practices and bureaucratic red tape. Although economic planners in the NIS claim to provide business-friendly environments and business practitioners seek MBAs and other advanced degrees, the implementation of effective business training programs is blocked by several challenges.

Challenges Confronting Belarusian Business Leaders and Educators

The establishment of independent republics such as Belarus, following the collapse of the Soviet Union and the disassembly of the command economy, has prompted enterprises in these transition markets to attempt to acquire western business practices. Many entrepreneurs and managers in the NIS are taking part in an economic and business transformation, a process that requires a shift in the very way economic activity is perceived and new critical skills consistent with western ways of doing business are implemented.

Developing an understanding of western business practices and culture by business and civic leaders in the NIS is dissimilar to mastering similar topics within the American environment. The transformation to a market economy manifests problems and complexities far beyond mere economic change. More than a decade after the Soviet break-up, the social, cultural, legal, political, and economic infrastructure needed to support a market system are still largely absent in the NIS. Facets of western business culture that we take for granted, such as an appreciation of the entrepreneurial spirit, a willingness to take risks, a respect for human rights, the importance of civic responsibility, freedom of speech, and the value of healthy dispute, disagreement, and compromise are often unknown.

The transition process has created stress, uncertainty, a significant reduction in the standard of living, and disillusionment to the very people who must now lead the needed economic transformation (Bennett 1996). These circumstances make learning an appreciation of western business practices and culture both critical and arduous. It is critical because without successful movement forward, the transition from a command to a market economy will stall or slide backward. It is arduous because of the political and cultural resistance to change and because what passes for business understanding in the NIS is often recycled communist economics and a twisting of western business reality. The view that the post-Soviet economic transformation would involve little more than replacing the command system with a market system was simply inadequate. Learning that conforms to a simple "slice" of market economics is devoid of the historical, cultural, political and institutional background needed to advance transition (Pickel 1995). The importance of understanding the culture and practices of both the West and the former Soviet system is a critical factor that must be carefully addressed if transition to a market system is to be successful, and if business training programs in the NIS are to be effectively implemented.

The residual effects of Soviet-style production systems and a dysfunctional command economy have spawned poorly developed accounting practices, with little understanding of fundamental principles such as operating costs, inventory management, budget analysis, and business planning. Marketing strategies, if existent, are often targeted toward non-existent customers, or even viewed as an unnecessary luxury for a cash-limited developing business. Team concepts, so prevalent in U.S. corporate circles, may be highly resisted by NIS entrepreneurs as a remnant of "cooperative" state-controlled enterprises of the past.

Young business professionals may lack Internet skills or access to computers, money is in short supply, and profit making can be a dangerous proposition, leading to excessive taxes, takeovers by the government, or even personal threats to business owners. Additionally, trust is a scarce commodity, and a guarded resistance to cooperation exists. There is little, if any, government support for business development. However, visions of a better future, coupled with an unusual patience for reaching goals, abound among young professionals.

Collaboration across national boundaries allows us to have a better understanding of differing cultural and political values and to strategize about the potential transfer of the Western-style business systems to the transitional economies in countries like Belarus. Classic business training programs, as practiced in U.S. business schools, may need to be refashioned to meet the special needs existing in Belarus and other NIS locales. Business educators, confronted by the formidable challenges inherent in translating western business practices into the realities of the Belarusian marketplace, must encourage a collaborative mindset that can lead to the development of a shared vision for a workable business climate in the NIS.

Collaborative distance learning offers an excellent tool for NIS educators as their countries move through the transition to a more democratic and diversified society. Cost-effective, collaborative distance learning projects can help to address the problem of limited educational resources and can prepare a new generation of business students who better understand the underpinnings of a democratic society operating in a free-enterprise system. In order to foster a more sustainable business climate in Belarus, business educators can use distance learning tools to tailor course material to account for cultural, social, legal and technological differences, to prepare prospective business students to become more receptive to western business practices, and to promote needed reform in infrastructure.

GOALS OF THE BRYANT COLLEGE CLD PROGRAM

An Internet-based CLD Program, linking Bryant College students and faculty, Rhode Island entrepreneurs, and leaders of non-governmental organizations (NGOs) with their counterparts in the NIS, was designed to address the administrative, educational and cultural challenges facing the business community in Belarus. The focus of the CLD program at Bryant is threefold: (1) to address the alignment of existing Belarusian educational practices with business development goals; (2) to introduce university faculty and undergraduate students to interactive learning techniques and collaborative mindsets; and (3) to train young Belarusian entrepreneurs and leaders from non-governmental organizations (NGOs) in western-style business practices.

OVERVIEW OF THE BRYANT COLLEGE/BELARUS CLD PROGRAM

To meet these challenges, a Bryant College faculty initiative was designed to address the educational climate for development of business skills in the NIS. The CLD Program serves as a model for bringing about change in educational style, communication competencies, and business practices in the republics of the former Soviet Union. Collaborative projects have included the following: (a) seminars on financial accountability for scientists and engineers who were formerly employed by the Soviet defense industry; (b) Web-based courses linking Bryant College, the European Humanities University (EHU), and the ENVILA Institute for Women in Minsk, and (c) a Summer School in Minsk on Collaborative Learning at a Distance. Other projects include a Rhode Island-based Community Connections Business internship program for visiting Belarusian and Ukrainian entrepreneurs, and the creation of a Center for International Collaboration (CIC) at the Information Technologies Center (ITC) of the National Academy of Sciences of Belarus. Some of these initiatives have been previously reported in the literature (Langlois and Litoff, 1999, Litoff and Ilacqua, 1999, Lux, 1999, Records, 1999, Langlois et al., 2001). The intent of this paper is to provide an overview of the goals, challenges and successes of the Bryant College CLD program, and to show how the lessons learned were utilized in the design of an exchange program for business entrepreneurs and NGO managers. These findings also serve as guiding principles for future cross-cultural collaborative endeavors. The linking of the different program components of the CLD Program are illustrated in Figure 1.

The collaborative projects in the CLD Program have utilized a wide array of information technologies, including the International Virtual Roundtable Discussion (IVRD) via E-mail, seminars on Web site con-

FIGURE 1. Links Among the Components of the Bryant College Collaborative Learning at a Distance (CLD) Program

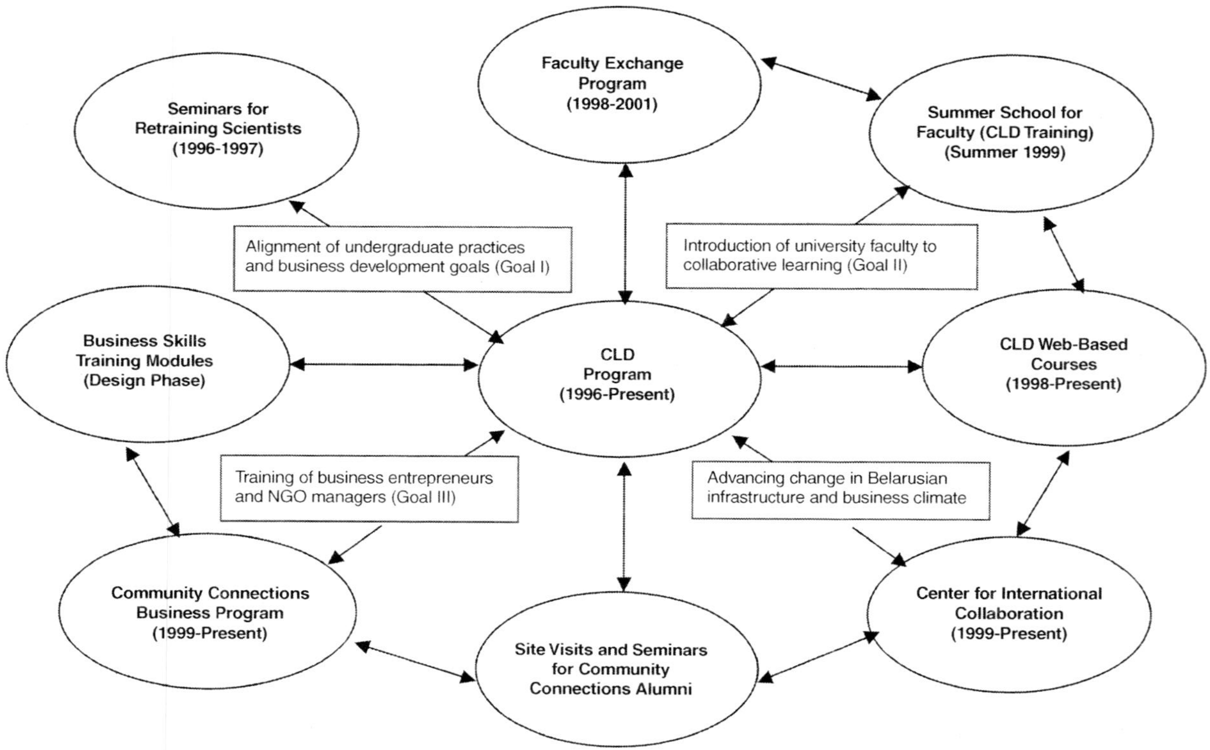

struction, Internet protocol video conferencing between the U.S. and Belarus, software training and development, and the use of the Internet to promote collaborative learning and open communication across cultural, economic, and political boundaries. This collaborative experiment has been led by scholars representing many academic disciplines, including economics, environmental science, history, management, mathematics, and computer information systems. The interdisciplinary nature of this Bryant College/Belarus alliance reflects the diversity found within global business settings, and has clearly contributed to the success of the program.

Underlying Educational Principles of the CLD Program

The ongoing CLD Program between Bryant College and Belarus focuses on a non-hierarchical model, emphasizing reciprocal, interactive learning (Dewey 1966, Johnson & Johnson 1996). At the center of our non-hierarchical model of learning is the belief that learning is a collaborative and active process, and that collaboration increases the opportunity for connecting with many different learning styles. Learners who take ownership of the learning process can be self-paced, and derive individualized benefits (Goodsell et al. 1992, Weiner 1992, Connick 1999, Oliver et al. 1998). Furthermore, reciprocal learning is fostered, aimed at encompassing all the actors within the learning process (Peters & Marshall 1998). A detailed discussion of this model and its application to the CLD Program was presented in earlier publications (Langlois & Litoff 1999, Langlois et al. 2001).

Non-hierarchical learning techniques, although common to U.S. educators, are relatively unfamiliar in university settings in the NIS (Hazell 1997). The interactive exchange of ideas between faculty and students is not commonly encouraged in the NIS, where a history of centralized education and strong governmental control over curricula has strongly influenced educational practice (Langlois & Litoff 1999). Even now, it is still uncommon for professors in the NIS to employ discussion, encourage questions from students, or design collaborative learning activities for their classes.

Also intrinsic to the CLD Program is the assumption that there is more than one pathway to learning. As noted by many observers, higher education is becoming more individualized, and technologically enhanced courses can support diverse learning styles (Altschuler 2001, Levine 2000). In recognition that learning is an interactive process, including exchanges among professors, students and informational sources, the Bryant College CLD program was designed to take advantage of electronic educational technology to accommodate differences in teaching/learning modes, cultural values, and communication styles.

Our Internet-based CLD Program is scaled to foster a personalized, interactive learning experience, which requires the teacher/mentor, student/learner, and all other stakeholders to become involved in the process, and committed to its success.

Given that team-based coaching and leadership skills will be required for effective functioning in the global marketplace, professors may find themselves acting as mentors and coaches to a much more diverse set of learners, located in distant geographic regions and possessing widely varying cultural backgrounds. In collaborative learning environments, students can also mentor each other, faculty can introduce conflict resolution skills, and human networking can be expanded (Langlois & Litoff 1999, Michaelsen & Black 1994, Webster & Hackley 1997). Collaborative learning allows students from diverse cultures to discover commonality, and thereby negotiate uncommon experiences more effectively.

Blending these ideas for collaborative learning in a non-hierarchical environment can lead to the creation of a "virtual classroom" (Langlois & Litoff 1999, Langlois et al. 2001). Since there are many pathways to learning, the virtual classroom, with its Internet and distance learning capabilities, can supplement activities within existing educational traditions, and serve as a precursor for future online and on-site business training programs in the NIS.

ALIGNMENT OF EDUCATIONAL AND BUSINESS PRACTICES IN BELARUS (GOAL I)

One of the critical elements of the Collaborative Learning at a Distance Program involves the concurrent teaching of interactive, Internet-based courses for Bryant and Belarus students. Like their Bryant counterparts, the student participants from Belarus are mostly preparing for careers in business, economics and law. Starting in the 1998-99 academic year, we offered three pilot courses to students in both countries: (1) The History of American Technology, (2) Cultures and Economies in Transition in the Post Soviet Era, and (3) Environmental Policy: Technology, Business and Government (Langlois & Litoff 1999, Litoff & Ilacqua 1999, Lux 1999). These courses, repeated many times, have provided a foundation for typical western-style business training programs at the undergraduate level.

Many pedagogical issues became clear during the initial offering of the courses. First, cultural differences significantly affected how students experienced the courses. Belarusian students enthusiastically completed readings and prepared written assignments, but seemed to miss the point of student projects that are so popular with U.S. students (Lux 1999). This observation underscores the implicit challenge of encouraging team-based activities that form the basis for current U.S. business practices. As recently noted, the most effective tool for integrating global business activities is the "cross-border team of individuals of different nationalities, working in different culture, businesses and functions, who come together to coordinate some aspect of the multinational operation on a global basis" (Govindarajan & Gupta, 2001).

Although a high level of energy was exhibited by Bryant students representing many countries and cultures, often accompanied by heated debates when students tackled the difficult challenge of understanding societies in transition, it was their shared common experiences as students that helped them negotiate their different perspectives. For example, during the Spring of 1999, E-mail exchanges of conflicting student perspectives about the Kosovo crisis took place (Litoff & Ilacqua 1999). This type of discussion demonstrates the value of exploring cross-cultural and comparative political differences in order to better understand complex global problems and comprehend diverse world markets.

Belarusian students, like Bryant students, are often poorly informed about the governmental infrastructure necessary to actualize well designed environmental and business policy, but the lack of transparency in governmental structure and practices in Belarus further complicates this problem. The process of acquainting Belarusian students with the roles that government and non-governmental organizations (NGOs) play in crafting environmental and business policy is difficult, even in the CLD setting. For illustration purposes, case studies and discussion of global issues seem to be more valuable than focusing on organizational diagrams of government infrastructure or lists of crucial U.S. legislation.

The concept of citizen participation in policy making is not well understood, and the idea of private business tackling basic infrastructure problems or forming public/private partnerships is dismissed as being totally unrealistic. Once more, it becomes clear that conveying basic business principles and describing citizen responsibility in a democracy may be more complex than might be expected. However, Belarusian students will be poorly equipped to face the challenges of today's globalization trends if they lack even a basic understanding of how government, NGOs, and businesses address environmental damage, encourage sustainable business practices, or meet minimal social needs.

Problems Encountered in the CLD Web-Based Courses

In implementing the CLD Program, we encountered many logistical and technical challenges. Although some of these problems have been previously described (Langlois et al. 2001), a summary of the most common problems is included here. Semester startup times are less consistent among Belarusian institutions, and may be quite different from academic terms at U.S. institutions, thus requiring adjustments to course syllabi and assignments.

Rarely are the required textbooks and supplementary educational materials for the CLD courses available in Belarus, even if students could afford expensive American textbooks. Each semester copies of all required textbooks and supplementary materials, including documentary videos, are made available to Belarusian collaborators, usually placed on library reserve. This practice helps to establish a culture of sharing academic resources. An additional problem involves the amount of reading that can reasonably be expected from Belarusian undergraduates who vary in English language skills.

Achieving quick and reliable access to the Internet is another challenge. Even now, navigating Web sites in Belarus can be slow and cumbersome, frustrating even the most patient users. To resolve this problem, we provide updated CD-ROM versions of the CLD course Web site to our Belarusian collaborators. The CDs can be used on computers connected to the Web in order to access hyperlinks. In addition, through the cooperation of information technology specialists at Bryant and EHU, a mirror Web site has been established. Clearly, familiarization with Web-based communication tools is an essential skill for today's business entrepreneurs, and funding for collaborative academic ventures must include technological upgrades and facility expansion for all participating institutions.

Synchronous E-mail communication between the United States and Belarus is not easily accomplished. While U.S. students are accustomed to daily E-mail messaging, most Belarusian students still have only limited access to E-mail. Belarusian students depend primarily on university computer laboratories, which may be equipped with new computer workstations, but the number of workstations seldom matches the number of potential users. Furthermore, most university students in Minsk do not live on campus, so considerable personal inconvenience may be involved. Although more Belarusian students are now taking advantage of the increased number of Web-based E-mail options, lack of access to a personal computer still limits E-mail use. Since it is inconceivable that business operations can be conducted in Belarus without easy access to the Internet and E-mail communication, the CLD Program experience points up yet another of the challenges facing business educators in Belarus.

Addressing the differences in E-mail writing styles of Bryant and Belarusian students represents an additional challenge for Internet-based course design. American students routinely display a casual approach to E-mail correspondence, often replete with coded abbreviations. By contrast, Belarusians usually create carefully constructed messages, thus exacerbating the time constraints caused by limited computer laboratory access. Again, these cultural differences reflect the complexities of communication in global business networks.

Time differences between the East Coast of the United States and Belarus (7 hours) present still another problem with E-mail communication. In order to encourage synchronistic E-mail communication with students, Bryant faculty adopted mid-day "E-mail office hours" that enabled us to avoid the busy use of the Internet in Belarus during the late afternoon, while still providing quick responses to Belarusian collaborators.

To promote and focus regular E-mail correspondence, we established the International Virtual Roundtable Discussion (IVRD) that prompts students to discuss assigned readings, special topics, and recent news, as well as promoting the sharing of cross-cultural and comparative perspectives. The IVRD was incorporated into all CLD courses, and was enthusiastically accepted by students and faculty at all participating institutions. At the completion of each discussion, a summary of the ideas discussed is posted on the respective CLD course Web site. This technique could be utilized for case study analysis or business problem assessment, as part of business training modules.

We occasionally use Microsoft's NetMeeting program to provide live, two-way, communication via the Internet. This program, standard on new computers, utilizes simple computer accessories (microphone, speakers, headset and small video camera) that avoid the high costs associated with long distance telephone charges and videoconferencing facilities (Langlois et al. 2001). However, time differences and limited facilities at EHU and ENVILA College for Women prevent frequent "net-meetings."

While the technical requirements of distance learning can be excessive, the Bryant/Belarus CLD Web-based courses were designed to be an inexpensive and modest project, affordable by most institutions. We avoid sophisticated software packages with extensive synchronous features that would necessitate our respective institutions to purchase and maintain additional software, and to offer the necessary training programs. The technological implications of the CLD courses have been discussed in more detail in previous publications (Langlois et al. 2001). Although the technological landscape has changed during the course of this program, access is still more limited for Belarusian students and faculty, as compared with Bryant and other U.S. institutions. By selecting the best and most cost-effective technologies suitable for the resources available in both countries, we have enhanced the equality of the partnership, and have made every possible effort to insure that technology remains a "silent partner." We have also attempted to use technologies that would be commonly used by global business partners throughout the world.

The interactions of students from different cultures and with different expertise and skill sets resulted in some interpersonal challenges, as well. Bryant students experienced anxiety when they were faced with the possibility of interacting directly with students from Belarus about that nation's transition issues, noting their lack of familiarity with Belarusian culture and economic realities (Litoff & Ilacqua 1999). Meanwhile, EHU faculty have reported that their students often feared that their English skills will be inadequate, or that their computer skills may not be as advanced as their American counterparts.

The design and delivery of lectures in Belarus by visiting U.S. scholars must take into account that, at best, Belarusian students will be using English as a second language, with varying skills. At worst, the ideas and concepts will be presented through an interpreter. Clear and concise ideation, presented in a deliberate manner, at a slower pace, is necessary to achieve maximal understanding by listeners. These skills can be mastered quickly by faculty and the payoff is instantaneous. Mastery of Russian is helpful, but not essential, because most of the coordinating faculty and students communicate reasonably well in English.

The challenges described above could pose serious impediments to the establishment of accredited joint undergraduate and graduate business programs between Belarusian and American universities. Furthermore, the Association to Advance Collegiate Schools of Business

(AACSB International/AACSB) would be likely to object to these arrangements if both institutions did not meet the assembly's accrediting standards. Additionally, AACSB requires a strong grounding in liberal arts at the undergraduate level. The CLD courses that we have introduced would help to provide the liberal arts foundation required by AACSB, and the lessons learned can serve as a road map for the development of collaborative undergraduate and graduate business programs.

Evaluation of CLD Web-Based Courses

In evaluating the Internet-based courses offered in the CLD Program, a Program Evaluation Checklist was developed, using standards endorsed by the American Federation of Teachers (AFT Guidelines 2000). Bryant College's CLD courses scored well on this checklist (Figure 2), meeting 13 of the 14 objectives, including the requirement for an "evaluation of successful and unsuccessful distance learning techniques."

A course assessment tool, designed to determine student response and satisfaction with Internet-based collaborative learning, was developed and distributed to classes at ENVILA Institute and EHU in the Fall 2000 and Spring 2001 semesters. Results indicated a general satisfaction with the program, particularly with respect to the interaction components of the course (see the Summary of Responses, Figure 3).

For example, most respondents "found a course of interest or value to me" and several respondents noted that the experience "fostered international collaboration between the U.S. and Belarus." Other respondents mentioned that the course enhanced their "skills in environmental studies and understanding of technologies for environmental protection" or that the course provided "training in English through Internet-based distance education." One section of the questionnaire queried respondents about "Problems to be Addressed in Future Courses" and respondents identified choices of subject matter for future courses (see Figure 4), including expansion of business course offerings.

Role of Faculty Collaborators in the Bryant College/ Belarus CLD Program

Selected faculty at EHU and ENVILA act as CLD course coordinators and are directly involved in the organization and implementation of the courses. On-site visits to Bryant and reciprocal visits to EHU and

FIGURE 2. Results Generated from Evaluating the Bryant College CLD Program

COLLABORATIVE LEARNING AT A DISTANCE PROGRAM EVALUATION CHECKLIST*

YES	NO	
X		Faculty retain academic control of courses and programs.
X		Teaching distance education courses is voluntary and results in positive recognition and/or additional compensation.
X		Training in technology is available for distance learning faculty.
X		Course design takes advantage of the many communication technologies.
X		Students understand course requirements, necessary time commitment, and have computer skills needed to succeed.
X		Faculty and students maintain close personal interaction.
X		Class size is set through normal faculty channels.
	X	Courses cover approximately the same material as included in traditional formats.
X		Courses in different subjects are offered.
X		Learning materials (articles, books, CDs, Web sites, etc.) were available to students.
X		Student assessment for comprehension and achievement was carried out.
X		Advising opportunities were available for students.
X		Faculty retain control over the use and reuse of distance learning materials.
X		Evaluation of successful and unsuccessful distance learning techniques was undertaken.

*Adapted from American Federation of Teachers "Guidelines for Good Practice in Distance Education."

ENVILA have helped to familiarize collaborating faculty members with technological needs, pedagogical philosophy, and procedural matters at each institution. These visits, ranging in length from a week to six months, have allowed collaborators to become familiar with one another's work style, special expertise, and cultural values (Langlois & Litoff 1999). As the Bryant/Belarus CLD Program has evolved strong connections among faculty, students, and entrepreneurs in the U.S. and Belarus have developed, resulting in shared research, collaborative training programs, and planned co-authored publications. This regular and personalized contact has been essential for trust-building and

FIGURE 3. Results Generated from Use of the CLD "Participant's Feedback Form"

Participant's Feedback Form

Profile of Participant:

0% Faculty
22% Graduate Student
78% Undergraduate Student

45% Highly motivated and participative
33% Attentive and moderately committed
22% Irregular participation due to personal scheduling difficulties

Language Skills:

67% Excellent English language skills (able to clearly express ideas)
33% Good to moderate English language skills (able to meet minimum reading and writing assignments)
0% Poor or limited English language skills (struggled to meet minimum requirements; had difficulty in understanding concepts and examples)

Computer Skills:

39% Good to excellent (mastered electronic communication goals)
61% Fair competency (met some communication goals)
0% Inadequate skills (need additional training)

Course Choices:

89% Found a course of interest or value to me
0% Need additional choices (if checked, give examples)
11% No response

Program Successes: (list)

- Shaping skills in environmental studies and technologies for environmental protection
- Communicating, sharing experiences, and making crucial decisions
- Training in English writing skills through Internet-based distance education
- Developing research skills; gaining experience in communication
- Learning from the U.S. experience in solving complicated environmental problems
- Incorporating innovative educational methods and approaches to higher education
- Making new contacts and sharing viewpoints
- Adding to theoretical knowledge
- Gaining an enhanced understanding of global problems
- Integrating an international experience into academic activities
- Realizing hidden personal capabilities
- Training in practical problem-solving, e.g., urban litter reduction
- Increasing computer literacy, promoting academic flexibility
- Fostering international collaboration between the U.S. and Belarus in academia

FIGURE 4. Problems to Be Addressed, as Viewed by Participants in the Environmental Policy: Technology, Business and Government CLD Course (Data taken from Participant's Feedback Forms)

Problems to be Addressed in Future Courses: (list)

- Economic growth as a result of environmental sustainability
- Development of ecological initiatives between the U.S. and Belarus
- Identification of the most controversial environmental issues of the 20th Century
- Political and economic aspects of environmental protection
- Raising an environmentally-conscious generation
- Costs of environmental pollution
- Costs and benefits of environmental protection programs; advantages and disadvantages
- Ecological NGOs in the U.S. and Belarus
- Environmental sustainability: governmental priority or public liability?
- Increasing public awareness of environmental studies
- Civic initiatives for environmental sustainability
- Moving toward global partnership through environmental sustainability
- Impact of environmental sustainability on economic development
- Causes and effects of soil pollution
- Psychological aspects of environmental pollution
- Impact of environment on social development
- Ecofeminism development
- Environmental sustainability in Third World countries (pro and con)
- Sea pollution and its aftereffects
- Oil production influencing human extinction
- Developing "Integrated Environmental Management"
- Impact of environmental pollution on women's health
- Nonproliferation of nuclear weapons
- Chemicals and the public; right to know
- Increased opportunities through environmental sustainability

Course with which I was involved:

Environmental Policy: Business, Technology & Government

shared vision, and for adding a sense of equality to the partnership. One of the reasons cited for the failure of global business teams occurs when "they are unable to cultivate trust among their members or when they cannot break down often formidable communication barriers" (Govindarajan & Gupta, 2001). The ongoing collaborations with our Belarusian partners have played a critical role in our ability to deliver the CLD Program, and to convey the importance of democratic traditions and government infrastructure in fostering a healthy business climate.

The success of the CLD Program has also benefitted from a strong liaison with the Information Technologies Center (ITC) at the National Academy of Sciences of Belarus (NASB). Through the efforts of Bryant faculty, who have developed close ties with key resource people at ITC and EHU, these distinctly different Belarusian institutions have bridged political boundaries to form a close working relationship between state (government-owned) and non-state (private) institutions.

Recognizing that business and commerce cannot flourish unless there is an open society marked by awareness of civic responsibility, and accompanied by a climate conducive to economic growth, European Humanities University and ENVILA College for Women have been pioneering in their efforts to introduce Western ways of teaching and thinking. EHU prides itself for its rigorous, modern curriculum modeled after western European and American institutions. ENVILA College for Women, like EHU, is dedicated to democratic traditions in an open civil society, and emphasizes the preparation of women leaders for the future development of Belarus. These universities have set forth a mission for transforming mindsets within their society, thus enabling graduates to better perform as responsible citizens and future business leaders.

By contrast, the ITC is a department within one of Belarus' oldest and most prestigious state-supported academies. This type of private-public partnership, common to U.S. business practice, is rare in Belarus, thus serving as an important model for future business endeavors. Possible applications of the private-public partnership model might include the development of recycling enterprises, or delivery of badly needed social services and health care.

Extension of CLD Program at Bryant College

The CLD Program amply demonstrates that Internet-based, collaborative courses can successfully address the educational needs of students at Bryant and at EHU and pave the way for more advanced business training. This has led to an expansion of distance learning projects between students at Bryant and Belarus in Microeconomics <*http://web.bryant.edu/~ec113jai*> and Macroeconomics <*http://web.bryant.edu/~jilacqua/ec114*>. In addition, the Environmental Policy: Technology, Business and Government course was extended to include students from China, interacting with students from EHU, ENVILA Institute for Women and from Bryant <*http://web.bryant.edu/~langlois/envpol*>. The course, Cultures and Economies in Transition in the Post-

Soviet Era, was revised and expanded to include utilization of collaborative Internet-based student projects from prior semesters as required reading *<http://web.bryant.edu/~history/h385nis/index.htm>*. Several faculty participants in the Summer School have acted as coordinators of these expanded course activities.

FACULTY TRAINING PROGRAM FOR CLD TECHNIQUES (GOAL II)

Bryant faculty collaborated with colleagues at the ITC and EHU to design a three-week 1999 Summer School, "Collaborative Learning at a Distance." This project introduced 25 faculty from Belarus and Russia to the theory and practice of collaborative learning at a distance, with the purpose of introducing western style educational practices to a greater number of university faculty. The creation of team-based Web site projects and the importance of using the Internet to foster economic growth in Belarus were also emphasized. Both EHU and the ITC provided classrooms, technical equipment, and expert personnel for the Summer School.

All Summer School participants engaged in E-mail roundtable discussions with other participants and faculty. Although many of the participants had never before used E-mail, they quickly achieved proficiency. An objective of the training program was to create an ongoing communication "web" wherein collaborators could benefit from a local support system, and maintain connections with the U.S. and Belarusian faculty.

Bryant faculty developed a comprehensive Web site for the Summer School, available at *<http://web.bryant.edu/~history/new/courses.htm>*. One of the most interesting features of this Web site, "Webbing and Web Page Workbook," was particularly helpful in guiding participants in how to break the linear mindset so common among academicians in the U.S. and Belarus. This section also included a tutorial on how to construct Web pages using the design tool, Netscape Page Composer, known for its ease of use by novice computer users, and standard on most new computers. Although newer versions of Microsoft Office provide a variety of Web-page design tools, Netscape Page Composer is commonly installed on both old and new computers, thus enhancing collaborative efforts across technology boundaries.

Collaborative Web projects were developed and published on the CLD Summer School Web site. Through teamwork, participants achieved high levels of technical performance within a short time frame. The development of Web sites by participants was an empowering experience that caused them to rethink their approach to collaborative teaching methodologies, information technology, and contemporary business practices.

Bryant faculty encountered some unexpected challenges during the Summer School, including the following: (1) marked differences in technical skills among participants; (2) limited Internet connectivity during classroom sessions; and (3) the unmet individual objectives of some participants with more advanced skills. Despite these challenges, the CLD Summer School far exceeded initial expectations, particularly the dedication, energy, and enthusiasm of participants. As a follow up, participants were given a CD-ROM version of the Summer School Web site, thereby assuring access to the Webbing tutorial and the collaborative Web projects. E-mail discussion groups were initiated, to foster continued communication among collaborators.

Evaluation of CLD Summer School

Web sites prepared by the Summer School participants were evaluated by the faculty coordinators, and were rated for content, graphic design, and webbing techniques. These evaluations are posted on the project Web site, so that all participants could benefit from the feedback. In addition, written evaluations were provided for each participant, addressing the level of commitment, quality of performance in the course, and improvement in Internet skills.

TRAINING ENTREPRENEURS AND NGO MANAGERS IN THE NIS (GOAL III)

The third phase of the CLD Program was initiated in the Spring of 2000, when Bryant implemented the first of a series of Community Connections Business Programs, funded by the U.S. Department of State. This program provides the opportunity for entrepreneurs from Belarus and Ukraine to visit the United States for month-long periods, collaborate with local businesses as interns, and meet with community leaders.

Three major objectives of the Community Connections Business Program exist: (1) to provide participants from the NIS with an opportunity to develop and enhance their skills in business management and operation, (2) to increase their knowledge base about American life and culture, and (3) to acquaint them with the practice of collaboration between public and private enterprises. Participants gain "hands-on" experience with the governance, operation, and interconnectedness among businesses, communities, local, state, and federal governments, and academic institutions. This is accomplished by means of professional seminars and workshops, internships, and site visits to cultural, governmental, educational, and business centers. This program addresses the needs, experience, and learning of entrepreneurs and managers from the NIS as they strive to make the transformation to commercial markets and western business practices and culture.

The operating paradigm of the Community Connections Business Program asserts that the new knowledge that is acquired helps to position both entrepreneurs/managers and their companies for success in commercial markets at home and abroad. Likewise, leaders of NGOs should become more skilled in developing effective service delivery systems, and bringing about necessary infrastructure changes to better realize their program goals. A Web site that accompanies the Community Connections program at Bryant and provides an avenue for continued participant interaction is available at *<http://web.bryant.edu/~comconex>*.

The selection process for participants in the Bryant College Community Connections Business Program includes a written statement of purpose for participating in the program, and evidence to demonstrate a good understanding of written and spoken English among the application materials. Interviews, initially held in Minsk, and later by telephone, are conducted in English and focus on a comparison of western business practices and economic policies with business practices in Belarus.

Participants in the program, including displaced scientists, educators, lawyers, and physicians, have described stress, uncertainty, and lowered standard of living as a result of the break-up of the Soviet Union. Participants have reported the absence of a social, cultural, legal, political and economic infrastructure needed to support a western-style market system, instability of the legal and regulatory systems, foreign distrust of the business environments in Belarus, insufficient knowledge of western business management practices, and inadequate business planning skills. Participants have also described themselves as pioneers, with few role models, networks or benchmarks in either the public or private sectors to draw upon for guidance.

In the first week of the Community Connections Business Program, two seminars are convened: (1) *American Dream: Myth or Reality*, and (2) *Management Issues for the 21st Century*, both designed to be interactive and broad-based and to acquaint program participants with the process of sharing diverse perspectives among different Bryant faculty members.

Internships with appropriate local business or non-governmental organizations are arranged for participants, to provide them with training, skills, and insights relevant to their own work in Belarus. Participant commentaries on their internship opportunities reveal the importance of this hands-on experience. One participant noted assistance in " . . . helping me better understand how to correctly organize my work in my company." Another wrote, "I felt like I'm a member of a great team." Participants also expressed an interest in the environmental protection regulations that were applied to American businesses, and emphasized that they hoped to apply their newly acquired skills to Belarusian businesses. Regarding financial accountability, an intern at a certified public accounting firm in Rhode Island noted that upon his return he would " . . . try to organize work with clients . . . based on financial documents of the client's company."

Application of lessons learned in the United States still remains fraught with challenges. One participant, upon returning to Minsk, successfully applied what had been learned about advertising, marketing and customer-friendly practices from her American Automobile Association internship to the camping and lodging business that she manages. The response of the Belarusian government was to nationalize the two most successful facilities. Another participant who manages a trucking company deliberately maintains a low profile in order not to attract the attention of the government, siting the company's repair facility outside the capital city of Minsk. This manager has also concluded that it is better to establish several small trucking companies than to have one company grow successfully and then possibly become a takeover target for the government.

By fall 2001, 50 participants from Belarus and Ukraine had completed this program. These face-to-face interactions have helped us to engage the Belarusian and Ukrainian business communities in an ongoing dialogue, and have better equipped us to coach participants in using collaborative techniques for productive networking in the global marketplace. In addition, the Community Connections program has encouraged greater communication between the academic and business communities in the NIS.

Evaluation of the Community Connections Business Program

In assessing the success of the program, it quickly becomes apparent that effectiveness cannot be measured by short-term results alone. The participants themselves recognize that the transformation of business practice and culture in Belarus will require the education, training, and experience of a new generation of Belarusians. However, they have also expressed that the eventual application of what they learned during their four weeks in the United States represents "great hope for Belarus and its future well being."

In August 2001, three Bryant College faculty visited Belarusian businesses and NGOs owned or managed by Community Connections Business Program alumni and coordinated seminars to discuss the impacts of the U.S. internships. The site visits took place in Minsk and Gomel, in Belarus, and encompassed a variety of businesses and NGOs. Feedback from alumni included a number of observations about the impact of the U.S. experience (see Figure 5).

As a direct result of these meetings and site visits, the program will be adapted to build upon successful activities, and to nurture the beginnings of business and NGO support networks in Belarus. The Community Connections Business Program Web site will be expanded to include updated contact information for alumni.

One follow-on activity associated with the Community Connections Business Program will involve the development of collaborative learning modules for alumni, addressing specific business problems confronted by these young professionals in a transitional economy, especially the tools that they need to compete in today's global environment. For example, these modules might include accounting practices or grant-writing skills for NGO managers, as well as topics such as managing conflict, expanding e-business opportunities, or developing public-private partnerships for business owners. Bryant faculty in each of the business specialties will be invited to work with the Community Connections Business Program alumni to design and implement these collaborative learning at a distance modules.

OTHER CLD PROGRAM INITIATIVES

Perhaps the most ambitious long-term outcome of the CLD Program will be the establishment of a proposed Center for International Collaboration (CIC) (Figure 6). We are working closely with the Information

FIGURE 5. Feedback from Community Connections Business Program Alumni

Benefits of Community Connections Business Program*

- Helped in revision of organizational structure (better planning, goal setting, and strategies)
- Changes in work style ("felt a moral imperative to change")
- Change in mindsets toward problem solving ("we can solve problems" or "each person can change society")
- Adapted U.S. business and infrastructure solutions to Belarusian settings
- Felt empowered to start new businesses
- Initiation of better networking skills; utilization of shared experiences
- Development of support networks with other alumni of the program ("a strong sense of community")
- Increased NGO partnering with other agencies and businesses; better funding possibilities
- Design of better marketing programs; improvement of public relations
- Better appreciation of Belarusian history and culture ("observed attitudes of Americans about their history")
- Need for expanded communication networks among Community Connections Business Program alumni
- Need for expanded business training programs in Belarus, tailored to meet specific needs of business managers in transitional economies

*Based on interviews and seminars conducted in Belarus, August 2001.

Technologies Center (ITC) at the National Academy of Sciences of Belarus to establish this Center, which will act as a business training center, focusing participants on the use of CLD techniques for training business and government leaders.

The CIC will be available to faculty, students, and researchers working at both state (government-owned) and non-state (private) institutions located throughout Belarus. The Information Technologies Center has already established training programs and set up technical conferences for scientists and decision makers in Belarus and other Newly Independent States, and has established on site training facilities for transforming ed-

FIGURE 6. Center for International Collaboration (Bryant College, Information Technologies Center (ITC) at the National Academy of Sciences of Belarus, European Humanities University (EHU), and ENVILA College for Women, Minsk, Belarus)

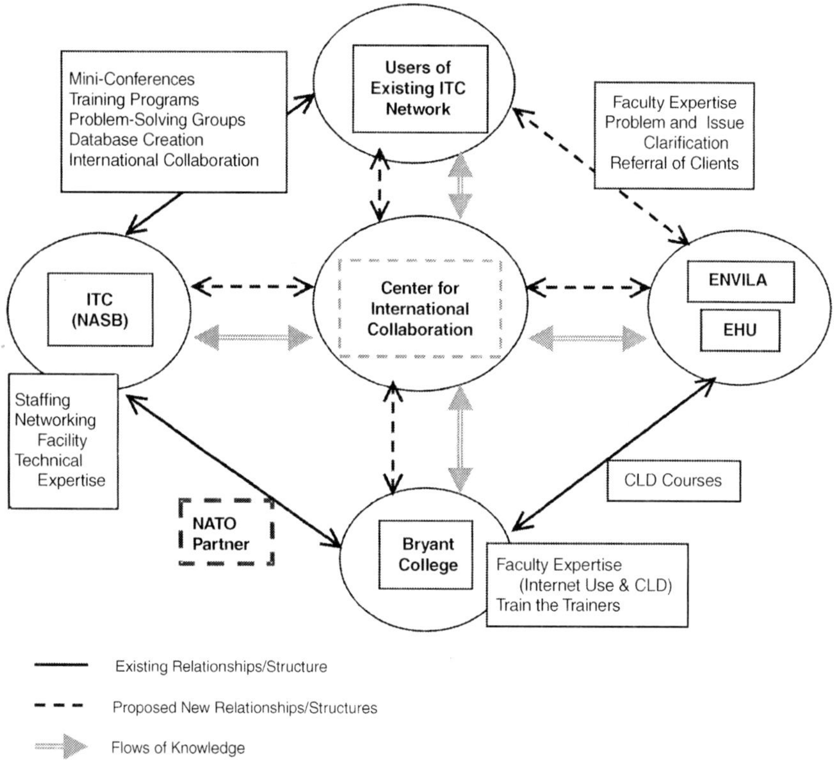

ucation in Belarus by using the technology and methodology of Collaborative Learning at a Distance. Students who take advantage of the Bryant/Belarus CLD Program therefore have the additional opportunity to become involved in national and international internships and CIC research projects. Distance collaboration tools provided at the CIC will enhance R&D efforts and facilitate virtual workshops where users can develop the necessary skill sets and knowledge for partnership development that will lead to global technology transfer projects and other joint business ventures. The CIC will also create opportunities for Internet users from the academic, business and scientific communities to become agents of change as they gain access to the global information system. Most importantly, augmented use of the Internet will foster expansion of cooperation among countries and enhance the discovery and dispersion of innovative opportunities and solutions to specific problems. In sum, the CIC will provide a forum for encouraging new partnerships of technical specialists and decision makers in the global R&D community and will act as a stimulus for business development.

CONCLUSIONS

The alliance of Bryant College with academic, business, and research institutions in Belarus demonstrates that Internet-based, collaborative learning across international boundaries, even with significantly different technological environments and requirements, can be achieved and supported by relatively inexpensive information technologies. Underlying the projects associated with the CLD Program is a commitment to collaborative approaches to decision making that makes regular use of cross-cultural analyses. The Bryant/Belarus CLD Program has also shown that Internet-enhanced courses and training programs that focus on collaborative learning, provide practical opportunities for academic, business, and research decision makers from the NIS to address regional challenges and to participate more fully in global markets.

REFERENCES

Altschuler, G.C. (2001, August 5). College prep: The E-learning curve. *The New York Times, Education Life Supplement*, 13-14.

Bennett, D.R. (1999, February). The stalled revolution: Business education in Eastern Europe. *Business Horizons*, 23-29.

Connick, G.P. (Ed). (1999). *The distance learner's guide*. Upper Saddle River, NJ; Prentice Hall.

Dewey, J. (1966). *Democracy and education*. New York: Free Press.

Going the distance: AFT guidelines for good practice in distance education. (2000, October). *On Campus*, 6-7, 23.

Goodsell, A.S., Maher, M.R., Tinto, V., Smith, B.L., & MacGregor, J. (1992). *Collaborative learning: A sourcebook for higher education*. University Park, PA: National Center on Postsecondary Teaching, Learning and Assessment.

Govindarajan, V. & A.K. Gupta. (2001). Building an effective global business team. *MIT Sloan Management Review*, *42*(4), 63-71.

Hazell, R. (1997). Exporting higher education: The Polish open university. *European Journal of Education*, *32*, 397-410.

Johnson, D.W. & Johnson, R.T. (1966). Cooperative learning and traditional American values: An appreciation. *National Association of Secondary School Principals, 80*, 63.

Langlois, G. & Litoff, J.B. (1999). Using a non-hierarchical approach to collaborative learning projects: The Bryant College model. *AABSS Journal, 2*, 9-17.

Langlois, G.A, Barrett Litoff, J. & Ilacqua, J.A. (2001). Reaching across boundaries: The Bryant College-Belarus connection. *Syllabus Magazine, 15*(3), 12-14.

Levine, A.E. (2000). The future of colleges: 9 inevitable changes. *The Chronicle of Higher Education, 47*(9), B10-B11.

Litoff, J.B. & Ilacqua, J.A. (1999). An overview of Bryant College's collaborative learning at a distance program with a progress report on teaching cultures and economies in transition in the post soviet era. *AABSS Journal, 2*, 2-8.

Lux, D.S. (1999). Teaching the history of American technology with Bryant College, European Humanities University, and Moscow State University students. *AABSS Journal, 2*, 18-23.

Michaelsen, L. & Black, R.H. (1994). Computer conferencing and collaborative learning: A discourse community at work. In Kadel, S. & Keehner, J.A. (Eds.), *Collaborative learning: A sourcebook for higher education* (Vol. 2, pp. 65-86). University Park, PA: National Center on Postsecondary Teaching, Learning and Assessment.

Oliver, R., Omari A., & Herrington, J. (1998). Exploring student interactions in collaborative World Wide Web computer-based learning environments. *Journal of Educational Multimedia and Hypermedia, 7*, 263-287.

Peters, J.M. & Marshall, J.L. (1998). Collaborative learning: People laboring together to construct knowledge. *New Directions for Adult and Continuing Education, 79*, 75-85.

Pickel, A. (1995). Official ideology? The role of neoliberal economic reform doctrines in post-communist transformation. *Polish Sociological Review, 4*, 361-375.

Weiner, H.S. (1992). Collaborative learning in the classroom: A guide to evaluation. In Goodsell, A.S., Maher, M.R. Tinto, V., Smith, B.L. & MacGregor, J., *Collaborative learning: A sourcebook for higher education* (pp. 89-96). University Park, PA: National Center on Postsecondary Teaching, Learning and Assessment.

Webster, J. & Hackley, P. (1997). Teaching effectiveness in technology-mediated distance learning. *Academy of Management Journal, 40*, 1282-1309.

Preparing the Human Capital for the New Millennium Using Information Technology

Rashmi Malhotra
D. K. Malhotra

SUMMARY. Information technology is transforming the economy at a breathtaking speed. The effect of technology on global business practices is profound and pervasive. These trends are changing and shaping the global economic landscape in the new millennium. These developments have major implications for the knowledge skills required for success in business in the information age. Students must be prepared for the challenges and opportunities that each of these trends represents. Therefore, the new knowledge economy demands changes in the models of global business education. Based on our experiences at our respective universities, this article describes how we are changing not only the way we teach, but also what we teach–as well as altering the way our universities do business. *[Article copies available for a fee from The Haworth Document Delivery Service: 1-800-HAWORTH. E-mail address: <getinfo@haworthpress.com> Website: <http://www.HaworthPress.com> © 2003 by The Haworth Press, Inc. All rights reserved.]*

Rashmi Malhotra is Assistant Professor of Management Information Systems, Saint Joseph's University, Haub School of Business, 5600 City Avenue, Philadelphia, PA 19131 (E-mail: rmalhotr@sju.edu). D. K. Malhotra is Associate Professor of Finance, School of Business Administration, Philadelphia University, School House Lane and Henry Avenue, Philadelphia, PA 19144-5497 (E-mail: MalhotraD@philau.edu).

[Haworth co-indexing entry note]: "Preparing the Human Capital for the New Millennium Using Information Technology." Malhotra, Rashmi, and D. K. Malhotra. Co-published simultaneously in *Journal of Teaching in International Business* (International Business Press, an imprint of The Haworth Press, Inc.) Vol. 14, No. 2/3, 2003, pp. 67-78; and: *Digital Technology in Teaching International Business* (ed: Lloyd C. Russow) International Business Press, an imprint of The Haworth Press, Inc., 2003, pp. 67-78. Single or multiple copies of this article are available for a fee from The Haworth Document Delivery Service [1-800-HAWORTH 9:00 a.m. - 5:00 p.m. (EST). E-mail address: getinfo@haworthpress.com].

KEYWORDS. Information technology, human capital, teaching, curriculum

INTRODUCTION

The growth of the Internet, globalization of trade, and the emergence of information economies, has recast the role of information technology in business and management. The Internet is becoming the foundation for new business models, new business processes, and new ways of distributing knowledge. Traditional firms are finding that they can use the Internet and networking technology to conduct more of their work electronically, seamlessly linking factories, offices, and sales forces around the globe. Companies such as Coca-Cola, Dell Computers, and Proctor & Gamble are extending these networks to suppliers, customers, and other groups outside the organization so they can react instantly to customer demands and market shifts wherever those occur in the world. When Coca-Cola corporate managers use information technology to examine their daily operations, they are able to find out exactly which bottling plant and which channels were used to sell Coca-Cola in a 500 milliliter bottle in any supermarket through out the world. This digital integration both within the firm and outside, from the warehouse to the executive suite, from suppliers to customers, is changing how we organize and manage business firms. Accordingly, these changes challenge and demand changes in higher level business education.

Alan Greenspan, the chairman of the Federal Reserve Board, in his speech to the U.S. Department of Labor National Skills Summit in February 2001, indicated that we are experiencing extraordinary economic innovation and are seeing its dynamic effects on productivity, real income, and job creation. But it is not enough to create a job market that enables those with few skills to grasp the first rung of the ladder of achievement. If we are to remain preeminent in transforming knowledge into economic value, the U.S. system of higher education must remain the world's leader. We must ensure that our whole population receives an education that will allow full and continuing participation in this dynamic growth market. This article profiles the demands of the knowledge-intensive economy, and discusses the suggested trends in business education. Further, the article also illustrates our experiences in understanding these initiatives–a case study of information technology (IT) pedagogical innovations at Saint Joseph's University and Philadelphia University.

MAJOR EDUCATIONAL OBJECTIVES

Four remarkable economic developments occurred in the past decade that have completely changed the face of business organization and business processes in the information age economy. First, after improving in speed, power, and convenience, the Internet has burst onto the economic scene. Second, the advanced economy has become so efficient at producing goods that most of the workforce has been freed up to offer services or to produce intellectual properties that are increasingly important to the economy, especially for information-intensive customized product/service. Third, consumers have been gaining market power and they are providing the direction, and impacting the pace of economic growth. Customized mass production has become the new mode of production. Besides customization, consumers are placing more emphasis on reduced cycle time. Fourth, the global economy has been enjoying a remarkable resurgence, particularly productivity growth. These developments have major implications for the knowledge and skills required for success in business in the information age. Knowledge about the strategic potential of IT and skills in using systems thinking and software tools are no longer the purview of IT specialists alone. For a firm's strategic goals to be achieved, managerial, marketing, financial, and accounting functions require IT–savvy managers and professional and IT–enabled processes. According to Dr. John D. Martin (2001), Baylor University's Carr P. Collins Professor of Finance, flexibility and rapid response are a key to success in the new Internet-driven economy for both businesses and business educators. Furthermore, Martin also predicts that the convergence of communication and information technologies have potential to revolutionize educational delivery system.

The new economy is forcing the education community to explore different ways of integrating IT into business education. Flynn and Kamm (1999) suggest integrating IT into business education at three different levels. The first focuses on creating infrastructures, the second on producing specialists, and the third on infusing IT into the business curriculum. Furthermore, besides enhancements in information technology, continued globalization of business and increasingly diverse workplaces also place more demands on the new technology-enabled education agenda (Harrison, 2000). In addition, to enable our workforce to reap benefits from technological advances, technologically advanced learning must be grounded in real-world curriculum that are relevant to changing business needs and offered in flexible, accessible values (Greenspan, 2001). McCorkle, Alexander, and Reardon (2001) present the diffusion of innovations theory as a process for accomplishing a more formal integration of discipline-specific technologies into a marketing and business program. Further, they also suggest the use of "technology champions" as a means of enhancing the technology diffusion process. Benbunan et al. (2001) propose the integration of information technology into the marketing curriculum of an undergraduate business program. They propose integration of IT via five technological modules:

1. Web-based communication among instructors and students,
2. Use of the marketing department's web site as an educational resource,
3. The Internet as a marketing medium,
4. Computer-supported market analysis and decision-making, and
5. Computer-enhanced business presentations.

In the information systems (IS) area, learning strategies can have a profound impact, because the IS field is changing rapidly. Drawing inspiration from both well understood traditional classroom learning and E-learning, King (2001) proposes an alternative learning model called the new classroom that draws from the experiences of both traditional classroom learning and E-learning, and demonstrates how an integrated educational strategy for IS can be developed. In fact, the Technology Education Committee in its report to the Association of Information Technology Professionals identified the exposure of students to computer programming as one of the essential elements. The report states that programming knowledge and experience is beneficial to everyone in an information society. According to Pietrykowski (2001), the introduction of computer-based technologies signals a new terrain of struggle over the purpose and nature of higher education. The computer-based instructional technology is ushering in a new era of labor market restructuring. The author critically assesses the current state of technological change, and offers Thorstein Veblen's insight into the purpose and structure of American universities. The Veblen analysis of the managerial model and its use by university administrators provide a remarkably cogent rendering of the present situation. What has changed is the use of computer-based technology to shift the balance of power in academe and to redefine the structure and content of higher education. During the past 20 years, corporate universities have migrated away from the ivy-covered academic institutions they emulated. Today, they more often consist of a partnership formed between an IT department and a local college to offer online training and distance learning company-wide. Traditionally, most corporate universities have concentrated their curricula on training junior and midlevel employees. However, a recent trend toward in-house executive education has led some companies to include a new emphasis on leadership development in their programs (Vitiello, 2001).

EXPERIENCING THE THRUSTS OF INFORMATION TECHNOLOGY

The continued growth of information technology has tremendous impact on today's global businesses and the need for workers who can manage vast amount of information (Frudling, Kerin, & Sebastian, 1997). Businesses need employees who recognize problems and use information technology to solve business problems (Breivik, 1998; Gregson, 1994; Morrison & Morrison, 1989; Secretary's Commission of Achieving Necessary Skills, 1991). Meanwhile, educators are criticized for not preparing students to solve the ill-structured types of problems faced in life (Brown, Collins, & Duguid, 1989; Hiebert et al., 1996; Stemberg, 1985). Embracing information technology in the classroom means far more than providing students with computer-driven cases and simulations. Current technology allows for a much richer experiential learning opportunity for our students. Classrooms should be modernized, computer-compatible and linked to the World Wide Web. Most business schools now provide an IT infrastructure so that teaching and learning can take place in a computer- and Internet-driven environment. Business schools should invest in high-tech classrooms, require laptop computers, port-per-pillow connections in dormitories, and wired lounges and study spaces. Recently, the Haub School of Business at Saint Joseph's University erected a new building where all the classrooms are smart rooms with computer, VCR, document camera, television, recording workstations, all bundled on one single podium. Further, to enable videoconferencing, the rooms are also equipped with smart chalkboards whose image can travel to the remote satellite campus sites and an additional projector sends the image of the students to satellite locations. Furthermore, faculty use "course info" web-based courseware to post syllabi, assignments, and examinations on the institution's intranet. The "course info" creates a personalized page for each student based on his/her enrollment for that semester. In addition, from last year onwards, the incoming freshman class is required to have a laptop computer so that all the courses can be techno-driven all the time, as opposed to the courses that are scheduled in computer laboratories. Creating online chat rooms and discussion groups using "course info" on the web encourages groupwork. More and more courses are delivered via distance education using videoconferencing. Saint Joseph's University is in the process of offering their Pharmaceutical MBA online. The entire curriculum will be delivered through online courses.

At Philadelphia University, to integrate technology in the curriculum, each faculty member is being encouraged to provide web-enhanced education by integrating assignments that require the use of World Wide Web. For instance, in finance courses, students are required to download foreign exchange rate data and interest rate data from the web site of the Federal Reserve Board to analyze the relation between interest rates and exchange rates. To make better use of their limited faculty resources, Philadelphia University offers foundation courses for the incoming MBA students online. Online courses enable students to learn in an interactive mode through threaded discussions and chat rooms. Offering foundation courses in an online mode has allowed Philadelphia University to use its full time faculty for core MBA courses. Students are tested through multiple-choice exams given online. The computer automatically grades the exams online. Furthermore, Philadelphia University is also offering a new online concentration in Textile and Apparel Marketing at the MBA level. The entire curriculum will be offered online with each course running for eight weeks and the curriculum emphasizes case studies specifically related to the textile industry and is targeted at non-U.S. students.

Also, recognizing the importance of changing technology and its impact on the business world and business education, Philadelphia University is offering a new undergraduate concentration in e-commerce. Students majoring in e-commerce are also being advised to select another functional area of business, e.g., accounting, finance, marketing, and international business so that they can be proficient in the applications of e-commerce to a specific functional area of business.

Infusing IT into the Business Curriculum

A complete level of IT integration must be achieved if students are to become successful business professionals for the information age. Especially with compulsory laptop computers at Saint Joseph's University, the main challenge is not the availability of the hardware and software, but complete integration of IT with the full range of all functional areas in the business discipline. While the MIS area can integrate IT in a natural manner, the other functional areas such as finance, accounting, and marketing pose a challenge. For example, in the area of finance, besides teaching financial systems, we integrate different software ranging from spreadsheet to neural networks and genetic algorithms. In accounting, to integrate business and information systems, we have used SAP modules. The marketing discipline has been completely revolutionized by new concepts of e-commerce and e-business, and new models of customer relationship management. The management area is integrating technology through new technological tools of project management, ERP planning and management, and change management. The production and operations management area focuses on service system design and implementation.

In addition to the IT-driven curriculum many schools offer a number of state-of-the-art technology-driven learning laboratories. These laboratories enable the infusion of IT into the business curriculum by providing students with a proactive use of business technologies and software along with a myriad of direct applications of theoretical concepts being learned in the classroom. For example, Bentley College offers numerous facilities such as a financial trading room, marketing technologies showcase, accounting center for electronic learning and business measurement, design, and usability testing center for their technically savvy student. Boise State University teaches network management hands-on with a student-run Internet Service provider. While formal approaches to network management may be covered extensively in lecture, it is very difficult for students to appreciate the importance and applicability of these concepts without experiencing them in practice. These special facilities offer a more realistic approach to teaching. As the students operate in a real-world environment, successes and failures are immediately evident in terms of services and customer satisfaction. Students are continuously balancing business opportunities and needs with technical capabilities and limitations. Students can experiment with new hardware, software, and systems. They draw into important realizations about the value of relatively simple and elegant solutions and the need to test new services on separate experimental system. Furthermore, these facilities offer collaborative learning opportunities, encourage students to make their own business and technical decisions, and increase student confidence level.

Finally, in this era of technological innovation, our education and training systems have felt the pressures of enlarging the pool of knowledge-intensive and technically savvy workers. Many schools have started offering techno-MBAs or master degree programs that integrate IT knowledge and business education. These programs seek to produce IT specialists with management skills. *Computerworld* now ranks the top twenty-five techno-MBA programs, based on surveys of recruiters and business school deans. These programs vary in structure and requirements. In many other MBA programs, students enroll in the institution's MBA program and select technology-related concentrations, such as computer information systems, information technology or management of technology. Graduates of these programs are in high demand, with starting salaries estimated to be 20 to 30 percent higher than those of other MBA programs. Therefore, as we proceed through the new millennium, it is time to re-evaluate the materials and methods that educators use to prepare business students for success in the workplace. Table 1 summarizes the pedagogical innovations that have come through as a result of infusion of information technology in curriculum in our respective universities.

REWARDS AND CHALLENGES

The information age has transformed the way people do business. Efficient operations are rewarded and required as never before. These changes should find their way into business school classrooms on consistent basis. The universities should provide a technology environment that is as current as possible. A major challenge most universities face is the investment in terms of equipment and support requirement to run these expensive programs. To provide our students with the talents necessary to compete in this marketplace, we must recognize and accept the challenges before us today. Offering technology-intensive curriculum is no longer a luxury. The complexities of information technology must be integrated into the core undergraduate and graduate educational framework. In addition, the educators themselves must embrace information technology as an opportunity to enhance educational efficiency. Furthermore, technology should also be a driving force for educational institutions themselves. For example, Saint Joseph's University like many other institutions uses a banner system and a campus pipeline to process information and is virtually going paperless. Activities such as getting class lists, posting grade sheets, registration for classes, employee services, salary information, etc., has all gone online.

TABLE 1. A Summary of Pedagogical Innovations

Infusing IT into Courses

- Finance: Use of Specialized software in teaching of Fixed Income Securities, Derivatives, Investments and Portfolio Management, Use of Internet to track bond prices, bond yields, stock prices, stock analysis, and exchange rate changes.
- Accounting: Use of business and information systems that includes SAP
- Marketing: Integration of courses in e-commerce and e-business
- MIS: Development of new courses in emerging technologies, e-commerce, and Internet technologies
- Management: Use of technology to illustrate business process management

Infusing IT into Programs

- New major in e-commerce at Philadelphia University
- Laptop initiative for the new incoming freshman class at Saint Joseph's University

IT Enabled Facilities

- New smart Internet ready classrooms at Saint Joseph's as well as Philadelphia University
- Smart Chalkboards
- Access to computers, document camera, and VCR in every class room

Curricular change also requires faculty members to learn and teach new materials and concepts. Therefore, another challenge universities face is to spend liberal funds on faculty development and retooling.

SUMMARY AND CONCLUSIONS

As computers and information technologies become more ubiquitous, one of the problems the business instructors face is how to integrate them into our classrooms and our students' lives. The continued growth of information technology has tremendous impact on today's global businesses and the need for workers who can manage vast amount of information. Businesses need employees who recognize problems and use information technology to solve business problems. As we enter the new millennium, it is time to re-evaluate the materials and methods educators use to prepare business students for success in the global workplace. International integration, innovations in information technology, mass customization, and the diversification of the American labor force continue to shape the landscape of tomorrow. This article outlines the challenges and demands of the knowledge-based economy, and discusses the course universities should follow in providing business students with the skills they need to succeed in this complex environment. Further, we illustrate our experiences in dealing with the advances in Information Technology from three major viewpoints–a general impact of information technology on business education, developing IT-infused curriculum, and the major rewards and challenges posed to universities. To illustrate these major IT pedagogical innovations, we draw from our experiences in embracing technology at Saint Joseph's University and Philadelphia University.

The convergence of communication and information technologies (such as the telephone, wireless, cable, Internet, personal computers, and television) has the potential to revolutionize the education systems as well as the education delivery system. While introducing and infusing information technology in business education presents many challenges, rewards, however, far outweigh the challenges. Business schools should face and prepare themselves in accordance with the new demands and opportunities of the computer age. The goal of business education is to educate students for a wide variety of technological and organizational contexts. Business schools should offer degrees that seek to manage behavioral and managerial dimensions with an interwoven technological curriculum in an IT-infused and telecommunication-driven environment. For faculty, such environments offer the best of both worlds: the ability to collaborate across great distances, and the ability to work in close collaboration on a personal level. In addition, to take full advantage of the technology, business schools should also not only change what and how they teach, but also how they themselves do business. Education has always been associated with people coming together to learn from the masters of a particular discipline. As organizations that are pure information enterprises, business schools should benefit the most from power of the information and technology revolution. In our viewpoint, there has never been a more exciting time both for business and business education.

REFERENCES

Benbunan-Fich, R., H. Lozada, S. Pirog, R. Priluck, and J. Wisnblit. (2001, April). "Integrating Information Technology into the Marketing Curriculum: A Pragmatic Paradigm." *Journal of Marketing Education*, 23, 1, 5-15.

Breivik, P. (1998). *Student Learning in the Information Age*. Oryx Press, Phoenix, AZ.

Brown, J., A. Collins, and P. Duguid. (1989). "Situated Cognition and the Culture of Learning." *Educational Researcher*, 18, 1, 32-42.

Dano, P. (1999, Autumn). "Lessons from History: Thoughts on the Future of Business Education," *Selections*, 16, 1, 1-4.

Flynn, P. and J. Kamm. (1999, Autumn). "Information Technology and Graduate Business Programs," *Selections*, 16, 1, 11-16.

Frueling, R., J. Kerin, and D. Sebastian. (1997). "The Information Age and its Impact on Business and Business Education Curriculums." *The Delta Pi Epsilon Journal*, 39, 2, 64-75.

Greenspan, A. (2001, February). "Investing in Human Capital," *Executive Excellence*, 18, 2, 9.

Gregson, J. (1994). "From Critical Theory to Critical Practice: Transformative Vocational Classrooms." In R.D. Lakes (Ed.), *Critical Education for Work: Multidisciplinary Approaches*, Ablex Publishing Corporation, Notebook, NJ, 161-180.

Harrison, D. (2000, Fall). "The Changing Face of Business Education: Challenges for Tomorrow," *Review of Business*, 21, 3, 43-46.

Hiebert, J., T. Carpenter, E. Fennema, K. Fuson, P. Human, H. Murray, A. Olivier, and D. Wearen. (1996). "Problem Solving as a Basis for Mathematics," *Educational Researcher*, 25, 4, 1221.

Jennings, L. (2001, July/August). "Teaching and Technology," *The Futurist*, 35, 4, 63-64.

King, W. (2001, Fall). "Developing an IS Education Strategy," *Information Systems Management*, 18, 4, 77-79.

Martin, J., (2001). The Carr P. Collins Professor of Finance, in a speech to Baylor University, Waco, TX.

McCorkle, D., J. Alexander, and J. Reardon. (2001, April). "Integrating Business Technology and Marketing Education: Enhancing the Diffusion Process through Technology Champions," *Journal of Marketing Education*, 23, 1, 16-24.

Minch, R.P. and S.W. Tabor. (2001, May). "Teaching Network Management Hands-On: Experiences with a Student-Run Internet Service Provider, *Decision Line*, 4-6.

Morrison, J., and P. Morrison. (1989). "Technology in Business and Changing Expectations," *Business Education Forum*, 46, 8, 3-6.

Pietrykowski, B. (2001, June). "Information Technology and Commercialization of Knowledge: Corporate Universities and Class Dynamics in an Era of Technological Restructuring." *Journal of Economic Issues*, 35, 2, 299-306.

Secretary's Commission of Achieving Necessary Skills. (1999). *What Work Requires of Schools–A SCANS Report for America 2000*, U.S. Department of Labor, Washington, D.C.

Sternberg, E., A. Baskin, and L. Hofer. (1986). "Organizational/Memory Tools: A Technique for Improving Problem Solving Skills." *Journal of Educational Computing Research*, 2, 2, 169-187.

Vitiello, J. (2001, April 9). "New Roles for Corporate Universities." *Computerworld*, 35, 15, 42.

Experiential Learning in International Business via the World Wide Web

Ilan Alon

SUMMARY. The article describes the implementation of Internet-based experiential projects within an international-business classroom setting and summarizes students' perceptions and attitudes towards the assignments. While the projects were shown to increase students' international business skills and abilities, students reported that the assignments were difficult and only mildly enjoyable. The paper discusses trends in business education and relates them to specific assignments designed to enhance learning outcomes. *[Article copies available for a fee from The Haworth Document Delivery Service: 1-800-HAWORTH. E-mail address: <getinfo@haworthpress.com> Website: <http://www.HaworthPress.com> © 2003 by The Haworth Press, Inc. All rights reserved.]*

KEYWORDS. Experiential education, project-based service learning, international business, WWW, Internet, cases

I hear and I forget, I see and I remember, I do and I understand.

–Confucius, c. 450 B.C.

Ilan Alon is affiliated with the State University of New York–Brockport, Business Administration and Economics, 350 New Campus Drive, Brockport, NY 14420-2914 (E-mail: ialon@brockport.edu).

[Haworth co-indexing entry note]: "Experiential Learning in International Business via the World Wide Web." Alon, Ilan. Co-published simultaneously in *Journal of Teaching in International Business* (International Business Press, an imprint of The Haworth Press, Inc.) Vol. 14, No. 2/3, 2003, pp. 79-98; and: *Digital Technology in Teaching International Business* (ed: Lloyd C. Russow) International Business Press, an imprint of The Haworth Press, Inc., 2003, pp. 79-98. Single or multiple copies of this article are available for a fee from The Haworth Document Delivery Service [1-800-HAWORTH 9:00 a.m. - 5:00 p.m. (EST). E-mail address: getinfo@haworthpress.com].

I. INTRODUCTION

This article tests the effectiveness of using an Internet-based experiential project (<www.globalview.org>) to augment learning outcomes in an international business class. The project has a number of advantages over traditional approaches of teaching international business:

1. It uses digital technology to communicate and disseminate information.
2. It is based on real-world–"live"–global cases.
3. It requires distributive collaborative learning.

The research uses a 16-item scale developed by Bobbit, Inks, Kemp, and Mayo (2000) to measure the perceptions of (1) the project's effectiveness as a learning tool, (2) how the exercise compares with more traditional types of instruction methods, and (3) general attitudes toward the project.

The paper is organized as follows. Section II describes three trends in business higher education: globalization, virtualization, and experiential education. Section III shows how Globalview (http://www.globalview.org) has been used to combine these trends in teaching international business. Section IV describes the experimental design and references three appendices related to the project. Section V summarizes the results, and section VI makes conclusions and recommendations.

II. TRENDS IN BUSINESS EDUCATION

Dramatic changes have been made in business education over the last two decades, primarily because of technological innovations and globalization. The Internet has facilitated the free flow of communication and the dissemination of information with little regard for national boundaries. Internet technologies have impacted business education in a variety of ways. At the same time, the last couple of decades have seen an explosion in international trade, international investment, and cross-border alliances. The virtual global village allows participants to emerge from remote corners of the world and interact with investors and educators alike. This section describes in detail three key changes that have developed in business education in recent years.

Globalization and Internationalization

The term "globalization" refers to the increasing integration and interdependence of nations across the world. In today's increasingly connected world, events on one side of the globe quickly send shockwaves throughout the world.

Consider the following statistics as illustrations:

- Twenty-five percent of everything made or grown in the world is exported.
- Foreign direct investment totals over $4.7 trillion (Ball et al., 2002).
- One billion people will be connected to the Internet by 2005 (Electronic Commerce Policy, 2001).
- It costs less than a $1 a minute to call just about anywhere in the world from the United States.

The cross-national exchange of ideas, people, money, goods and services forms the basis for the globalization of markets and the internationalization of firms. Increasingly, competition, employees, partners, suppliers, and buyers will come from overseas.

Businesses have long complained that colleges and universities are not adequately preparing students for entry into the working world. For international companies, hiring people who can function effectively and efficiently transnationally is a challenge. As a result, international businesses have very low expectations of formal education and rank experience as more important for ultimate job performance. To combat these perceptions, Webb, Mayer, Pioche and Allen (1999) suggested that schools use internationally experienced faculty and an interdisciplinary international business curriculum which embodies cross-cultural education. In order to maintain U.S. competitiveness, the AACSB asks that member business schools require all business majors to take international business courses and internationalize all their other business courses, focusing on the global implications of their respective areas.

According to international business employers, the key characteristics of top International Business programs are:

- Language training,
- Overseas internships,
- Student foreign-exchange programs, and
- Case studies of real I.B. problems (Webb et al., 1999).

The present research focuses on this last and shows how technology can mitigate physical distance.

The Internet, the World Wide Web, and the Virtual Classroom

The Internet has been used by academics in a variety of teaching and learning formats. Some universities have begun to offer entire curricula or parts of it over the Internet. Classes utilizing traditional brick-and-mortar lecture formats are also utilizing the Internet in a variety of teaching, research and testing formats. Atwong and Hugstad (1997) noted six areas that can benefit from increased use of the Internet: lecturing, designing instructional material, mentoring individual students, evaluating student performance, recruiting majors, and facilitating student collaboration.

Writing about the development of a web-based, Internet marketing course, Kaynama and Keesling (2000) specified a number of generally applicable advantages of Internet-based applications over traditional lecture and textbook approaches. The Internet is more dynamic and can embody multimedia capabilities that capture and maintain audience awareness and interest for longer periods. Hypertext capabilities act as navigational facilitators that are non-linear, constructivist, and free of the contextual constraints often imposed by textbooks.

One need not see the Internet as replacing traditional teaching formats, but as complementing and enhancing traditional formats by adapting to new paradigms of learning. Alon and Cannon (2000), for example, have constructed an International Business website to complement a global case research project for the dual purposes of enhancing students' information-gathering skills and developing technology-usage abilities.

Faculty inclusion of technology into the classroom is often gradual and incremental. It tends to start with the use of e-mail correspondence to communicate and consult selected students, ending with the virtualization of all course elements. Many instructors seek a balance between web-based and class-based presentation of material. Concerns still exist, however, over connectivity, system reliability, institutional constraints, and the technical deficiencies of students and faculty.

Institutions of higher education have realized the value of integrating technology into curricula. Some have set up instructional technology centers whose sole purpose is to disseminate instructional technology around campus–motivating, teaching, listening, and collaborating with faculty. Brahm (1997) suggested that the on-line delivery of education presents substantial barriers to entry including developmental costs, learning and training costs, hardware requirements, and system software costs.

Experiential Education

An increased demand, from students and practitioners alike, for experiential learning has accompanied the increased use of in-class technology. Although it is simplistic to suggest a direct relationship between the increasing availability of data on the Internet and the push for a more practicum-based undergraduate model of business education, there is nonetheless some relationship between the two. Under pressure from businesses, colleges and universities have begun to respond by attempting to give students practical experience, such as internships and service learning programs.

The development of "real world" skills and abilities in the curriculum is still in its infancy. Experiential learning programs, both within and outside the class, have the potential to sharpen the types of skills that businesses seek. Simply defined, experiential learning is "learning by doing." In this way, students integrate new skills into their ways of thinking by practicing new behaviors. As the opening quote makes clear, this is not a novel pedagogy.

A number of organizations have been established to support this growing trend in international business education, an increased focus on experiential education. For example, the National Society for Experiential Education (NSEE) and the Association for Experiential Education (AEE) are membership associations that (1) embrace experiential learning in the classroom, workplace, or community; and (2) promote experiential education in all settings and support professional development, theoretical advancement, and evaluation in experiential education worldwide (NSEE, 2000: AEE, 2000). The AEE motto, echoing Confucius, is: "Tell me, and I will forget; Show me, and I may remember; Involve me and I will understand" (AEE, 2000).

Another experientially based organization that focuses on free enterprise is Students in Free Enterprise (SIFE), a non-profit organization whose mission is "to provide college students the best opportunity to make a difference and to develop leadership, teamwork, and communication skills through learning, practicing, and teaching the principles of free enterprise." SIFE has teams on more than 700 colleges and universities across the U.S. and in 13 other countries.

There are many types of experiential learning: field-based experiential learning versus classroom-based; simulation-based versus real companies; historical case studies versus "live" case studies; highly structured versus loosely structured. The global case program discussed below is a *classroom-based, "real," "live," and loosely structured case study.*

While internships provide excellent adjuncts to business education in general, internships have been slow to react to the growing need for globalizing the curriculum and are mostly domestic and local in nature (Toncar and Cudmore, 2000). Internships cannot be easily integrated into traditional classroom formats.

A number of scholars, such as Burnard (1989), Joplin (1981), and Kolb (1984), have argued that experiential learning is superior to traditional methods. Experiential learning requires active participation; it is student-based; it allows students to build on subjective evaluations and perceptions; it is inductive and explorative. The net effect according to proponents of experiential learning is that students become more interested and engaged, retain the information better and for longer periods, and learn how to apply otherwise elusive theoretical constructs.

To make undergraduate education in business more effective, Bobbitt et al. (2000) proposed the integration of experiential learning exercises across the business curriculum. Working in teams, students in Principles of Marketing classes created products and promotional materials that were featured in a mock tradeshow; students in Personal Sales and Sales Management classes selected products from the tradeshow they wished to use to complete a sales call. These researchers suggest that the integration of experiential teaching methods across the curriculum enhances student learning outcomes.

Gremler et al. (2000) proposed that experiential learning assignments in Business classes are more likely to develop students' interpersonal and communication skills, understanding of course concepts, teamwork and team building, listening skills, and critical-thinking and problem-solving skills.

Despite the growing trend of globalization, classroom-based experiential learning in international business courses has received little attention in the literature. It is difficult to experience a different culture during the course of a semester, so experiential aspects have been underplayed. To some degree, the Internet has bridged the traditional distance barriers for experiential learning in international business. For example, virtual tours of foreign countries and foreign companies are already possible.

III. ASSOCIATION GLOBAL VIEW

Association Globalview (AGV), through its Internet site <http://www.globalview.org>, features two types of experiential business programs: a simulation program and a global case program. The Global Cases Program was developed as an outgrowth of the simulation program; it is the focus of this article. It is unique because it focuses on "real" and "live" cases of firms seeking to internationalize. Unlike the simulation program, global cases do not require matching calendars for all participating faculty and schools, a task difficult to achieve in an international setting.

Association Global View was born in 1996 out of a collaboration between California State University Chico (CSUC), *Ecole des Practiciens de Commerce International* (EPSCI), and The Amsterdam School of Business (HES). The collaborative project was an international business simulation that brought students from each university into competition via distance education. By the beginning of 2001, more than 5,000 students from 25 universities representing 12 different countries had competed in the simulation. Although this program provided the foundation for the Global Cases Program, it will not be discussed in detail here.

In 1999, a number of faculty members from CSUC began to consider the current AGV Global Cases Program as it might relate to live cases in the classroom. They began developing cases relating to specific companies seeking internationalization and, through solicitation, were joined shortly thereafter by business faculty in other areas of the country and the world. By 2000, 83 faculty members from 18 countries[1] in the Americas, Asia, and the Middle East had signed up to use the program. This widespread diffusion occurred because the program is innovative and is available for free to professors and students both. However, most of the participating professors did not fully integrate their classes into the Global Cases Program because there is a high learning curve and because full installation of this technology in the classroom was viewed as risky (often the case with the implementation of any technology). Still in its infancy, the Global Cases Program has a dedicated, core group of professors that have learned to use the program, are active in its development, and have worked to refine the concept.

Global Cases is an online system that allows clients (businesses and entrepreneurs) a direct connection to the academic community. These clients benefit from the program by increasing their knowledge and capability base, being able to identify potential future employees, developing links with local universities, and receiving free consultation. Businesses, however, need to be actively involved with students to provide them with guidance and needed information. Such involvement may be costly and distracting, taking the attention of managers from other pressing issues. In order to lower the cost to the firm and maximize the benefit of the final reports, projects are directed by faculty members in participating schools, who mediate between the firm, the students, and AGV administrators. It is currently the responsibility of professors to obtain cases, manage the program on-line, and require students to use the system; however, professors are allowed to use existing cases developed by others.

Global Cases is experiential, focusing on small and medium-sized companies that seek internationalization. The Internet allows students to post status reports, read about the specifics of assigned cases, communicate with each other, and download and upload relevant reports. Using project-based service learning, students develop international business plans for interested businesses. Alon and Cannon (2000) have observed the use of global cases in teaching international marketing at the State University of New York College at Oneonta. They have concluded that four key student-learning outcomes emerged from the projects: (1) increased content knowledge of tendencies in international marketing, (2) increased information management skills, (3) measurable increases in Internet and technology management skills, and (4) increased collaborative teamwork and communication skills. Similarly, other instructors using Global Cases at the Chico campus of the California State University have reported that the project gives students (1) "real-world" collaborative experience; (2) the ability to be active participants, creating new knowledge; (3) global learning exercises; and (4) hands-on practice with a variety of information technology media and media delivery systems (Davis and Schlais, 2000). In short, AGV facilitates student learning by requiring teamwork skills useful in the identification of solutions for those practical international business problems faced by small and medium businesses in today's global economy.

Schools also tend to benefit from student involvement in AGV through increased involvement with local business communities, developed public awareness of university contributions, and heightened reputations for developing unique educational programs utilizing practical experience. In one college utilizing AGV, a local newspaper reported student achievements and suggested that these student-led projects would help local economic development (*The Daily Star*, 1999). These same claims were echoed later in the university's public relations efforts via Sawchuk, Brown and Associates.

While it is a lot of work to coordinate and administer, professors benefit from the Global Cases Program by decreased potential plagiarism (since each assignment is unique), enhanced student-learning outcomes and interest, and innovation in curriculum design and technology implementation in the classroom. Such efforts are usually recognized by college administrators and are likely to be rewarded during tenure and promotion time.

IV. EXPERIMENTAL DESIGN

This study reports on the students in an introductory international business class at the State University of New York (SUNY) College at Brockport who constructed international business plans for local (NY-based) and international (Chinese and Mexican) firms which expressed interest in internationalization. Appendix I shows a sample case outline for a small, NY-based, high-technology firm. Students were divided into groups in the beginning of the semester and each group was assigned a "live" case to analyze during the semester. The final assignment was to create a case-specific international business plan using an instructor-developed, loosely structured outline.

The project is loosely structured and is done mostly out of class, with the instructor acting as a facilitator and a coach. Students are faced with an ambiguous situation that they need to research for the first time, controlling the process and outcome of the assignment. According to Hamer (2000), in such unstructured assignments students need a longer period of time to first learn the material and then creatively apply it to solve "real world" business issues. Loosely structured experiential activities have been shown to increase student enthusiasm and satisfaction (Lawson, 1995; Dabbour, 1997), grades (Perry et al., 1996), and the perceived value of education (Graeff, 1997).

When the project was originally conceived, the final assignment was unstructured and students were forced to cooperate with another student-team from a cooperating school. Instead of following an outline, students were asked to evaluate the company's situation and to work with its executives to develop firm-specific solutions. Students were given little direction and were easily frustrated with the whole process. Thus, an outline was developed and sample cases from previous semesters–stored on AGV in electronic form–were provided for students to model. Appendix II shows a generic final assignment outline related to the global cases.

After engaging the students in the above-described experiential exercise for a semester, we wanted to measure the learning outcomes for the first time in order to systematically evaluate what students thought about the project. To do that, we used an established instrument, developed by Bobbit et al. (2000). This 16-item scale was used because it measures the perceptions of (1) the project's effectiveness as a learning tool, (2) how the exercise compares with more traditional types of instruction methods, and (3) the general attitudes toward the project. See Appendix III for the scale. Because this is exploratory research, we followed the example of Bobbit et al. (2000) and have reported the descriptive statistics (shown in the next section).

International business at SUNY Brockport is a required course for all business majors, primarily populated by juniors and seniors. In total, two sections of this course which were taught during the same semester (Spring, 2001), in an identical way, by the same professor were used as the sample for the study. Students were instructed on how to search for international business data using the Internet and using the library's resources both by the instructor and by a librarian early in the semester, enabling them to find case-relevant information.

A total of 55 students completed a questionnaire at the end of the semester (28 and 27 students in Class 1 and Class 2, respectively). The questionnaire is reproduced in Appendix III. In order to maximize student participation, the questionnaire was administered right before the final exam when student attendance was almost perfect. We followed this procedure to minimize non-attendance bias and to gain insight from the entire class.

V. RESULTS

Table 1 contains the results of our study for the entire sample and for each of the two classes separately. Class 1 was a day class, while Class 2 was taught at the same college–though at a different campus–by the same professor, during the same term, but it was offered once a week in the evening. Other identifiable differences between the two classes are summarized in Table 2.

The questions were factored into several dimensions: *enjoyment* (V2, V4, V8, V10, V11), *group-work* (V6), *comprehension and international-business skill development* (V5, V7, V12, V14), *difficulty* (V15

TABLE 1. Student Attitudes Toward I.B. Experiential Project

	Class 1 + 2	(n = 55)	Class 1	(n = 28)	Class 2	(n = 27)
	Mean	SD	Mean	SD	Mean	SD
V1: More productive than lecture	3.69	0.92	3.71	0.94	3.63	0.97
V2: More enjoyable than lecture	3.22	1.10	3.39	1.13	3.00	1.07
V3: More productive than other projects	3.38	0.87	3.43	0.88	3.30	0.91
V4: More enjoyable than other projects	2.87	1.00	3.96	0.96	2.81	1.00
V5: "Real world" understanding	3.93	0.88	3.86	0.80	3.96	1.02
V6: Working collaboratively in a group	3.65	1.04	3.82	0.95	3.59	1.01
V7: International business understanding	3.85	0.85	3.79	0.92	3.85	0.95
V8: Career in international business	2.80	0.99	2.86	1.04	2.74	0.94
V9: Should not be re-assigned in future	2.38	1.24	2.50	1.23	2.26	1.26
V10: Best part of the course	3.04	1.14	3.29	1.24	2.78	0.97
V11: More interesting than term paper	3.95	1.00	4.21	0.88	3.70	1.03
V12: Confidence in I.B. skills	3.93	0.92	4.11	0.83	3.81	0.83
V13: Not worth the effort	2.33	1.07	2.43	1.20	2.26	1.02
V14: I.B. concepts understanding	3.84	0.88	3.86	0.84	3.81	0.92
V15: Work hard at learning vs. listening	3.40	1.05	3.36	1.03	3.44	1.08
V16: A great deal of effort into project	4.80	0.40	4.86	0.36	4.78	0.42

Scale: (1) strongly agree to (5) strongly disagree

TABLE 2. Differences Between Class 1 and Class 2

Class 1: Day Class	Class 2: Night Class
Met 3 times per week	Met once a week
86% would recommend the course	100% would recommend the course
Mostly Juniors	Mostly Seniors
Reported 3.7 hours of homework per week	Reported 4.0 hours of homework per week
Mostly traditional students	Mix of traditional and adult students
Suburban Campus (Brockport, NY)	Urban Campus (Rochester, NY)
Mostly full-time students	Mix of full-time and part-time students

and V16), and *productivity* (V1 and V3). Two negatively worded questions were also used to validate the results (V9 and V13).

On average, students mildly enjoyed the project with an average rating of 3.18 (3.0 is a neutral position), gained an appreciation of what it takes to work in groups (3.65), developed international business skills and abilities (3.89), worked extremely hard to complete the assignment (4.10), and were slightly more productive then they would have been in a traditional lecture or project environment (3.54). The negatively worded questions were, as expected, lower than 3.0 (with an average rating of 2.36).

VI. CONCLUSIONS

The project described in this paper is a proven success in terms of learning outcomes and student-reported perceptions. The companies involved benefited from international business plans that can be used to identify selected countries for expansion. The school enjoyed several benefits from its collaboration with the business community: at the very least, the program enhanced the learning environment and provided students with "real-world" skills and abilities that they should be able to reproduce for their potential employers.

Professors who wish to keep their students up-to-date and trained for the labor force may want to institute the concepts of globalization, technology and experiential learning into their classroom teaching/learning activities. The case explored in this article embodies these three important trends–it focuses on internationalization, utilizes the Internet, and develops student skills through teamwork and customized projects.

Professors need to adjust to the changing paradigms of education, but not necessarily discard traditional methods of teaching. Table 3 shows the differences between traditional and new learning environments. Learning occurs by a combination of thinking, feeling and doing (cognitive, affective and behavioral learning styles). Different learning styles are appropriate for different parts of the curriculum, and different

TABLE 3. Changing Paradigms in Business Education

	Traditional Paradigm	"New" Paradigm
Delivery	Lecture–Chalk	Experiential/Interactive
Focus	Teacher–Centered	Student–Centered
Teaching Style	Telling	Coaching
Student Involvement	Passive Listeners	Active Participants
Theory versus Practice	Theory–Laden	Experience–Laden
Learning Style	Memorization	Application
Learning Process	Deductive	Inductive
Understanding	Objective	Subjective
Development	Information Dissemination	Skill Development
Grading Basis	Individual	Group
Tests	Multiple Choice	Written and Oral Presentations

students have different preferences and processing abilities. Therefore, this article suggests that teachers incrementally introduce "new" paradigm methods, testing their acceptance and adjusting them to students' needs and preferences.

The introduction of such methods will inevitably be resisted by some students who do not want to immerse themselves in the subject and who wish to limit their educational experience to lecture attendance and multiple-choice examinations. The project described in this article necessitated a great deal of coordination among team members and many hours out of the classroom searching and researching questions and issues never explored before. It was, thus, accompanied by various student complaints such as: "we don't know how to do it," "it is too difficult," "we cannot find any information," "we are lost," "there isn't enough time." Such perceptions can lead students to downgrade the usefulness of the assignment and to reject the educational delivery system. The role of the professor in such instances is to provide students with guidance and structure and to give them direction on information selection and retrieval. Professors experimenting with experiential education should be ready to contend with resistance to change. The rewards are great, however, when students and teachers find diverse ways to interact with each other and the outside world.

NOTE

1. Australia, Canada, United States, Netherlands, Belgium, South Korea, Austria, United Kingdom, France, Switzerland, Kuwait, Singapore, Spain, Sweden, Argentina, New Zealand, Ireland, and Israel.

REFERENCES

Alon, Ilan and Nancy Cannon (2000). Internet-Based Experiential Learning in International Marketing: the Case of Globalview.org. *Online Information Review*, 24 (5), 349-356.

Arenson, K. (1998, December 16). SUNY Board approves core courses. *The New York Times*, 5.

Association for Experiential Education (1999). Retrieved August 24, 2000 from <http://www.aee.org/>.

Association of College and Research Libraries. (2000). Information Literacy Competency Standards for Higher Education. Retrieved September 5, 2000 from <http://www.ala.org/acrl/ilcomstan.html>.

Atwong, Catherine T., and Paul S. Hugstad (1997). Internet Technology and the Future of Marketing Education. *Journal of Marketing Education*, 19 (3), 44.

Ball, Donald A., Wendell H. McCulloch, Paul L. Frantz, J. Michael Gernger, Michael S. Minor (2002). *International Business: The Challenge of Global Competition*. New York: McGraw-Hill Higher Education.

Beck, S. (1997). Evaluation Criteria. The Good, The Bad & The Ugly: or, Why It's a Good Idea to Evaluate Web Sources. Retrieved September 5, 2000 from <http://lib.nmsu.edu/instruction/evalcrit.html>.

Bobbitt, L. Michelle, Inks, Scott A., Kemp, Katie J, Mayo, Donna T. (2000). Integrating Marketing Courses to Enhance Team-Based Experiential Learning. *Journal of Marketing Education*, 22 (1), 15-25.

Burnard, P. (1989). *Teaching Interpersonal Skills: A Handbook of Experiential Learning for Health Professionals*. London: Chapman & Hall.

Canzer, Brahm (1997). Marketing Education on the Internet: A World Wide Web Based Introductory Marketing Course Design For the Virtual Project in Distance Education at Simon Fraser University. *Journal of Marketing Education*, 19 (3), 56-66.

Class Makes Plans for Firms. (December 16, 1999). *The Daily Star* (Oneonta, NY), 2.

Dabbour, Katherine Strober (1997). Applying Active Learning Methods to the Design of Library Instruction for a Freshman Seminar. *College and Research Libraries*, 58 (July), 299-308.

Davis, Richard and Dennis Schlais (2000). Learning and Technology: Distributed Collaborative learning Using Real-World Cases. California State University at Chico, Working Paper.

Electronic Commerce Policy (2001). The Emerging Digital Economy: The Digital Revolution. Retrieved September 3, 2001 from <http://www.ecommerce.gov/danc1.htm>.

Fardouly, N. (2000). Learning Styles and Experiential Learning. Retrieved August 24, 2000 from <http://www.fbe.unsw.edu.au/learning/instructionaldesign/styles.htm>.

Graeff, Timothy R. (1997). Bringing Reflective Learning to the Marketing Research Course: A Cooperative Learning Project Using Intergroup Critique. *Journal of Marketing Education*, 19 (Spring), 53-64.

Gremler, Dwayne D., K. Douglas Hoffman, Susan M. Deaveney, and Lauren K. Wright (2000). Experiential Learning Exercises in Services Marketing Courses. *Journal of Marketing Education*, 22 (1), 35-45.

Hamer, Lawrence O. (2000). The Additive Effects of Semistructured Classroom Activities on Student learning: An Application of Classroom-Based Experiential Learning Techniques. *Journal of Marketing Education*, 22 (1), 25-35.

Joplin, L. (1981). On Defining Experiential Education. *Journal of Experiential Education*, 4 (1), 17-20.

Kolb, D. A. (1984). *Experiential Learning: Experience as the Source of Learning and Development*. Englewood Cliffs, NJ: Prentice Hall.

Lawson, Timothy J. (1995). Active-Learning Exercise for Consumer Behavior Classes. *Teaching of Psychology*, 22 (October), 200-202.

National Society for Experiential Education (2000). Retrieved August 24, 2000 from <http://www.nssee.org/intro.htm>.

Perry, Nancy Walker, Matthew T. Huss, Bradley D. McAuliff, and Julie M. Galas. (1996). An Active-Learning Approach to Teaching the Undergraduate Psychology and Law Course. *Teaching Psychology*, 23 (April), 76-81.

Quick, Don (1998). Experiential Learning in Higher Education. Retrieved August 24, 2000 from <http://www.colostate.edu/orgs/ctlearn/forums/handouts.html>.

Sullivan, D. (2000). Web Searching Tips. Retrieved September 5, 2000 from <http://searchenginewatch.com/facts/index.html>.

Toncar, Mark F., and Brian V. Cudmore (2000). The Overseas Internship Experience. *Journal of Marketing Education*, 22 (1), 54-64.

Webb, Marion S., Kenneth R. Mayer, Virginie Pioche, and Lida C. Allen (1999). Internationalization of American Business Education. *Management International Review*, 39 (4), 379- 397.

APPENDIX I

Sample Case Outline Alon Electronics, Inc.

STAGE OF DEVELOPMENT

Feasibility Study; Market Development

AREAS OF INVESTIGATION

International Business

International Marketing

Business-to-Business/Government Marketing

CASE DIFFICULTY

Medium to High

OBJECTIVES

- Seek out additional export opportunities in foreign markets.
- Identify potential target-markets for Alon Electronics in the import country.

APPENDIX I (continued)

- Develop a list of potential customers and distributors in the import market.
- Determine the need to direct and adapt promotional materials.

DESCRIPTION OF COMPANY

Alon Electronics is a "make-to-order" business (i.e., a job-shop) for a very small niche in the electronics marketplace: high-voltage mica-paper capacitors and electronic modules (SIC Codes 3675, 3679). It has a low-volume, high-variety product mix. The main products are bespoke (i.e., custom-made) mica paper capacitors, Teflon film capacitors, polymer film capacitors, electronic modules, etc.

The manufacturing cost per unit varies with each part. It depends on the amount (and type) of materials, the amount of labor, etc. The company competes successfully in the market by offering high-quality, high-reliability, customized products embodying high levels of technology.

DESCRIPTION OF MARKET

Alon Electronics customers include aerospace, satellites, oil and gas drilling companies as well as defense contractors and electronics distributors.

International sales account for approximately 15% of total sales. The company currently exports its products to Australia, Austria, Canada, France, Germany, Israel, Italy, Japan, Norway, Sweden, and the United Kingdom. The company has nine domestic and five international manufacturing representatives (U.K., Germany-Austria, Israel, Canada, and Italy).

DELIVERABLES

The target semester concentrated on the following countries:

MERCOSUR countries: (1) Argentina, (2) Brazil, (3) Paraguay, and (4) Uruguay as well as associate members (5) Chile and (6) Bolivia

East Asian Tigers: (1) Malaysia, (2) Singapore, (3) Taiwan, (4) Indonesia, and (5) China

Analyses included:

Economic Variables

1. GNP and multi-year trend
2. Defense budgets and multi-year trend
3. Inflation and growth rate
4. Deficits and deficits as percents of GNP
5. Exchange rate and multi-year trend

Political Variables

1. System of government
2. Conflict and/or cooperation with the U.S.A.
3. Attitudes toward foreign business

Demographic Variables

1. Population size and growth

Social Variables

1. Similarity to the U.S.
2. Language and English literacy
3. Education level

Competitive Variables

1. Relative labor costs (compared to the U.S.)
2. Size and strength of competitors
3. Electronics industry trends

Electronics-Related Sectors

- Identify potential programs/projects, customers, government information and cultural characteristics that impact the following industries in the country:

1. Aerospace
2. Defense
3. Oil and Gas Drilling
4. Satellites (communication, defense, etc.)

APPENDIX II

Final Assignment Outline

Cover Page (Participant's name, group number, company, and region)

Executive Summary (Key point of the report in one page)

Table of Contents (with page numbers)

I. INTRODUCTION

What company, what countries, what will you talk about in the rest of the paper?

II. AN EXAMINATION OF CHOICE OF COUNTRIES

What are the key drivers of demand in your industry (relevant variables)?

What country was chosen and why? Tables with references.

III. COUNTRY ANALYSIS

Environmental analysis of selected country with a table.

Analysis of opportunities and threats.

IV. CHOICE OF MODE OF ENTRY

Your choices:

- Exporting Entry Modes
  - Indirect
  - Direct
- Contractual Entry Modes
  - Licensing
  - Service Contracts
  - Management Contracts
  - Turnkey Operations
  - Co-production Agreements

Investment Entry Modes
- Joint Venture (new establishment/acquisition)
- Sole Venture (new establishment/acquisition)

Explain why you decided to go with your chosen mode of entry. Remember that companies prefer low levels of internalization, risk and control when they are small, are relatively inexperienced, and when market conditions are turbulent.

V. IDENTIFY POTENTIAL PARTNERS, DISTRIBUTORS, AND CUSTOMERS

Create a list with full contact information if possible.

VI. CONCLUSION

Create a diagram detailing the steps that your company needs to take to sell its products abroad.

APPENDIX III

Questionnaire

<http://www.globalview.org>

1	**2**	**3**	**4**	**5**
Strongly Disagree				Strongly Agree

1. As a learning experience, this project was more productive than listening to a lecture.
2. As a learning experience, this project was more enjoyable than listening to a lecture.
3. Compared to group projects in other business-related courses, this project was more productive.
4. Compared to group projects in other business-related courses, this project was more enjoyable.
5. My understanding of "real-world" problems and opportunities improved as a result of this project.
6. As a result of this project, I have a greater appreciation of what it takes to work in a group.
7. My understanding of international business was enhanced by this project.
8. This project has stimulated my interest in pursuing a career related to international business.
9. This project should not be assigned to future classes.
10. This project was one of the best parts of the course.
11. Compared to writing a term paper, this project was more interesting.
12. Having completed this project, I am more confident that I could complete this type of project for a company.
13. The learning experience provided by this project was not worth the effort.
14. My understanding of the concepts of international business was enhanced by completing this project.
15. This project gave me stronger motivation to work hard at learning than listening to lectures does.
16. I put a great deal of effort into this project.

Teaching Business Strategy for an Emerging Economy: An Internet-Based Simulation

Van V. Miller

SUMMARY. An Internet-based simulation about a business in an emerging economy is presented and described as a crucial ingredient for a business strategy course dealing with emerging economies. The development of the course took place in three separate classes where experiments were conducted regarding the key ingredients necessary for a course designed to teach Business Strategies for an Emerging Economy. The simulation, when coupled with today's dominant strategy paradigm, the Resource Based View, appears to yield a course design that attracts students while emphasizing the actual substance which is crucial in such a course.

KEYWORDS. Teaching, business strategy, emerging economy, Internet, simulation, resource based view

INTRODUCTION

In the summer of 1998, approximately 25 faculty members (including this author) from around the United States attended a workshop

---

Van V. Miller is affiliated with the College of Business, Texas A&M International University, Laredo, TX 78041 (E-mail: vmiller@tamiu.edu).

[Haworth co-indexing entry note]: "Teaching Business Strategy for an Emerging Economy: An Internet-Based Simulation." Miller, Van V. Co-published simultaneously in *Journal of Teaching in International Business* (International Business Press, an imprint of The Haworth Press, Inc.) Vol. 14, No. 2/3, 2003, pp. 99-114; and: *Digital Technology in Teaching International Business* (ed: Lloyd C. Russow) International Business Press, an imprint of The Haworth Press, Inc., 2003, pp. 99-114. Single or multiple copies of this article are available for a fee from The Haworth Document Delivery Service [1-800-HAWORTH 9:00 a.m. - 5:00 p.m. (EST). E-mail address: getinfo@haworthpress.com].

highlighting a unique Emerging Economies Simulation, now Internet-based and hereinafter referred to as the Simulation. It had been developed by faculty in the Kellogg Graduate School of Management at Northwestern University with support from the U.S. Department of Education. The author's interest in the topic had been piqued because he had just attempted to teach, using a fairly standard approach, a business strategy course for Latin American economies to a group of MBA students. The pedagogical frustrations of that initial experience provided the impetus for participating in that workshop, which has provided some of the key ingredients needed for a successful learning experience in an emerging economies course.

Based on the workshop and the author's experiences as discussed below, those key ingredients are: (a) *general and specific information about the particulars of emerging economies* or the contrasts between such economies and the more developed, capitalist economies; (b) *knowledge about the business strategy concept*; and, (c) *an integrative experience* that allows the students to tie the relevant information and knowledge together. To use a metaphor from geometry, each key ingredient represents one side of an equilateral triangle with sides a-b-c (see Figure 1). The triangle itself symbolizes a solidly *constructed model* for an emerging economies course.

The sides symbolize not only the necessary structural ingredients for a successful emerging economies course, but they also indirectly reflect the author's three "experiments" in teaching the course. Each experiment has used the ingredients, or better said the substance found in each ingredient, as a treatment effect. Those experiments or teaching experiences form the empirical base and represent the conceptual grounding for this article.

FIGURE 1. The Emerging Economies Course Triangle

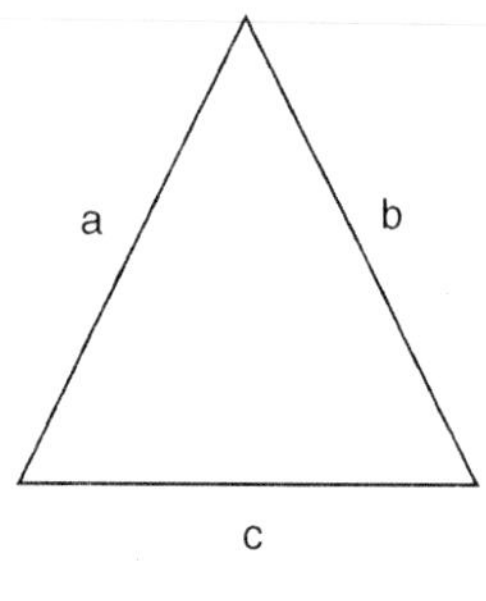

Before describing those experiments in the next section, two of the three key ingredients, due to its breadth and complexity, general and specific information about the particulars of emerging economies will not be a major focus of this article, require initial clarification vis-à-vis the Simulation. In the Simulation–an integrative experience for the emerging economies course–the user not only experiences the complicated difficulties of introducing baby food into a former Soviet Union republic, but he/she also realizes the challenges of learning to use the Simulation itself. Such challenges are understandable given the need to create a teaching simulation that can realistically represent the often chaotic situation found in an emerging economy. The Simulation *with its interactive capability* does quite adequately recreate the circumstances surrounding that situation. However, to develop that setting and then to give the student the skills for analyzing it, the Simulation's creators had to construct a number of abstract strategy instruments that can overwhelm the normal student in his/her first experience with it.

The instruments themselves are not alien or contrary to prevailing knowledge about the business strategy concept, but that fact is not easily discernible to most MBA students, especially if the emerging economies course does not require strategic management as a prerequisite. For the students, there can appear to be two very distinct and separate sets of concepts about business strategy–one for developed countries and another for developing countries. Clearly the external context of each is different, but contextual differences do not necessarily require different analytical concepts that are intellectually divorced from one another. Assuming a neo-liberal model for the global economy, which the Simulation does assume, contextual differences can be examined with the same basic analytical instruments of strategic management. Such an examination must allow for the much higher degree of uncertainty found in an emerging economy, but the Simulation accomplishes that quite well. In light of this integrative pursuit, the author has decided to link the instruments of the Emerging Economies Simulation with the dominant concepts of business strategy. Pedagogically, the conceptual linkage offers the student a more coherent and consistent view of strategic management and can reduce the level of learning uncertainty within the course itself.

The value of using a simulation for teaching the complexity of international business can be found in the work of Jenkins (1998), McGraw and Palmer (1999), and Ruhe and Allen (2001). Though the latter two studies stress the usefulness of simulations for teaching cultural matters, the earlier work of Wolfe (1993) clearly indicates that they can be utilized in numerous settings where complexity is found. Such a setting is that of the emerging economy which Kaynak and Kucukemiroglu (1997) focused on in a more traditional approach in their development of the curriculum for a marketing course in a developing country.

The manifest purpose of this article is twofold: (1) to introduce international business professors to an exciting and valuable Internet-based teaching method that offers an integrative experience for the emerging economies course, and (2) to confront the challenge of linking the analytical instruments of the Emerging Economies Simulation to prevailing knowledge about the business strategy concept. After discussing in the following section three experiments or exploratory attempts to teach emerging economies, the article then provides a brief summary of the Simulation and its instruments. In the fourth section, those instruments are examined from a business strategy perspective and positioned appropriately within the Resource-Based View (RBV). Finally, the author, based on his experiences with the Simulation, summarizes the challenges encountered in using it and notes particularly the difficulties that he has uncovered while utilizing it with a group of MBA students whose primary language is not English. Dealing with the language obstacle seems quite germane if, as educators, we desire to provide a first-rate business education not only to the students of the First World but also to the students of the Third World where the emerging economies are quite real and not a mere abstraction.

THREE EXPERIMENTS IN TEACHING AN EMERGING ECONOMIES COURSE

Recognizing the rising importance of emerging economies and given the author's area specialization in Latin America, a special topics course, *Business Strategies for Latin America*, was offered to MBA students during the spring term of 1998. The MBA program was a small one at a regional university on the Gulf of Mexico. The enrollment of just nine students in the special topics course was considered more than adequate for this particular MBA program. Students self-selected to enroll in the course and cannot be considered representative of the student population. The format of the course was constructed around a set of diverse readings and discussions about the business strategy concept, an aggregation of readings, videos, cases, talks, and discussions over Latin American countries, and a course project focusing on a San Antonio-based telecommunications company that had made major inroads into that industry in several Latin American nations. Looking back at this initial endeavor to provide a business strategy course on emerging economies, the author can easily discern the three sides of the emerging economies course triangle.

However, the substance represented by two of the sides was problematic in that it created confusion for the students. Side b, *knowledge about the business strategy concept*, was too general and overarching. The students were overwhelmed by all the ideas and tools that are contained in the vague and evolutionary notion of strategy. As a field, it seems to shift paradigms about once each decade and to myopic view, the latest paradigm Is the ultimate paradigm. Even strategy scholars cannot agree on a core paradigm for the field (see Mintzberg, 1995, regarding the basic disagreements within strategic management, or Gilbert, 1992, for a stinging rebuke of the field's direction). Given that the course was not intended to be a doctoral seminar in the nuances of strategy theories and concepts, the author/professor often found himself engaged in the task of explaining subtleties irrelevant to this particular course. The confusion was even worse for the students who had not yet taken the capstone, strategic management course.

The triangle's side c, *an integrative experience*, was contained in the course project with the telecommunications company. The experience with the corporate managers was quite enjoyable and highly interesting, but their information did not mesh well with side b–*knowledge about the business strategy concept*. As just noted, it was confusing to many of the students, and it did not resonate with the words used by the managers. In addition, because the telecommunications market was in the process of being opened up through privatization in many Latin American countries, the managers were not able to speak about much industry-specific material that was still considered confidential. Thus, it was at times impossible to link the strategy concepts with particular country information. In summary, the first experiment revealed the need for *an integrative experience* which would directly link the substance of the *knowledge about the business strategy concept* with the *general and specific information about the particulars of emerging economies.*

The Emerging Economies Simulation appeared to offer exactly that link. It is an integrative experience with abundant information about a particular, though hypothetical, emerging economy along with details about a specific industry in that country, and it is rooted in business strategy concepts. The author had occasion to implement the Simulation with another group of MBA students at the same university in the spring of 2000. These 19 students were enrolled in the required capstone policy/strategy course and had spent most of the semester learning about corporate and business strategy through the book, *Corporate Strategy: Resources and the Scope of the Firm*. The book's authors, Collis and Montgomery (1997), are both from the Harvard Business School and have written a text with cases that presents a balanced (i.e., it does not jettison the Industry Structure Model) perspective of the Resource-Based View (RBV). It became the dominant strategy paradigm in the 1990s and is still in vogue. After studying this material for some twelve weeks, the students were asked in the final two weeks of the course to link it to the first two decisions in the Simulation.

The better students had few difficulties in relating the RBV to the baby food situation found in the Simulation; however, the other students struggled with the task and complained about insufficient time to complete the project. Their complaints were probably legitimate. The Simulation does require the comprehension of a lot of material. First, the user must read and understand the complicated situation facing the company as it enters a new national market. Then, the student must figure out and apply the strategy process stipulated in the Simulation to the major decisions that must be made in order to enter and compete in the new market. For the average MBA student, mastery of the Simulation's situation and process within two weeks presents a considerable challenge, and when it is coupled with the strategy concepts of the RBV, it can be an overwhelming, though positive, experience.

In this second limited experiment, the author also noted that the students had scant appreciation for the problems found in an emerging economy. For example, the Simulation's mention of political unrest and a potential civil war did not appear to concern the students. They simply assumed political stability in their decisions. To understand this, one can refer to side a of the triangle–*general and specific information about the particulars of emerging economies*. The Simulation provides such information, but it does not and cannot sensitize the students to comprehend and apply information of this nature. In summary, the second and more constrained experiment indicated that: (1) the Simulation is capable of providing *an integrative experience* if sufficient time is allotted to it, (2) *knowledge about the business strategy concept* is within the Simulation though relating it to the RBV can be problematic for most students, and (3) the Simulation cannot teach students to appreciate and then apply some of the *general and specific information about the particulars of emerging economies*.

In the spring term of 2001, the author had the opportunity to conduct his third experiment at teaching an emerging economies course to 18

MBA students. Regarding the students, the major differences were their university and nationality. The university is located on the Mexico-Texas border, and the students were predominantly Mexicans enrolled in a Spanish MBA program with classes conducted in Spanish but materials, with few exceptions, in English. The course was again a special topics class, *Business Strategies for Latin America*, but with more emphasis on Mexico. This course, as the first one, relied on readings, cases, videos, and discussions about business strategy concepts and Latin American particulars. In addition, the author/professor lectured on the RBV and thereby offered the students the rudimentary knowledge needed for tying it to the strategy concepts used in the Simulation and the course project. Because of the Mexican emphasis in the course, the Simulation with its own specific tools was used not only as an end but also as a means that allowed the students to integrate their course learning in that context as well.

The results of this third experiment indicated the following (again, there was a very positive reaction to the Internet-based experience) in reference to the key ingredients:

a. a dedicated course does teach and sensitize students to *general and specific information about the particulars of emerging economies* although Mexican students hardly needed sensitization to such matters;
b. such a course can offer *knowledge about the business strategy concept* though confusion still abounds (perhaps aggravated by the language obstacle) due to the myriad notions about the concept; and
c. the Simulation clearly provides *an integrative experience* that can, if so desired, be utilized to augment other integrative experiences in the course.

In light of the three experiments, the biggest challenge facing a professor in an emerging economies course is the one that deals with *knowledge about the business strategy concept*. That challenge is best addressed after explaining the specifics of the Simulation.

THE EMERGING ECONOMIES SIMULATION

As already noted, the Emerging Economies Simulation was developed by faculty at the Kellogg Graduate School with U.S. Department of Education support. Their industrial collaborator on the project was Motorola University, and the Simulation in its entirety can be viewed at <www7.kellogg.nwu.edu/emerge>. A user will need to contact the site administrator in order to register a class and to secure a password. In the introduction to the Simulation, they state that it was *designed to complement coursework and help users learn the complexities, trade-offs, and dynamics of emerging economy conditions and operations through hands-on experience. Decisions must be made with limited and sometimes conflicting information. Underlying and interrelated factors are highlighted and users see the impact of incorrect assumptions. Unlike in a standard case, conditions will change and new information (including discovery of facts not previously recognized) will become available even as users are developing recommendations.* With this intended design or purpose in mind, the faculty over time developed the Simulation that is currently available and will be reviewed next.

The fictitious company that the student users are consultants to is Henzger, a multinational producer and seller of baby food. The name is a combination of Heinz and Gerber, but the students are advised not to use either as a model for their decisions. The country that Henzger intends to enter is Cheroca, a former Soviet republic in eastern Europe with some resemblance to the Ukraine (again, it should not be the model). After analyzing all the information available (within the Simulation there are numerous documents plus expert opinions provided), the student consultants are asked to undertake three assignments that are reports to Henzger's managers who must then make the necessary decisions with commitments for entry into Cheroca's baby food market.

The three assignments along with the Emerging Economy Planning Toolset (to be described below) are the strategic instruments found in the Simulation. The assignments can be summarized as follows:

Assignment One–It concentrates on an analysis of the strategic fit or alignment between Henzger and Cheroca. The student consultants are asked to address questions about the company's objectives, orientation, capacities, strengths, and weaknesses. At the same time, they must also assess Cheroca's interests, flags or areas of concern, legacy, and resources. In evaluating Henzger and Cheroca together, the students are requested to identify the resources, internal and external, that will be needed to sustain a competitive position in the national market.

Assignment Two–Building on the first one, it requires the users to examine the three strategic options, two joint venture candidates and one acquisition possibility, that are open to Henzger for its entry into Cheroca. Tools needed for this analysis are *assumptions, flags, scenar-*

ios, and *roadmaps* that allow the student consultants to see how their strategic plan is beginning to look. In developing the strategic plan, the students are pointedly asked to think about it in terms of competitive position and the resources and capacities necessary for sustaining that position. When examining the three strategic options, there is a suggestion that each option be scrutinized from the perspective of scenarios, i.e., new developments that could seriously affect that particular option. Anticipating the next assignment, the users are told to begin development of a basic roadmap for entry into the country.

Assignment Three–This task rests on the previous one and assumes moving ahead with the entry into Cheroca; however, it implies unanticipated events there that will seriously impact the preferred strategic choice for entering Cheroca. Such events, caused by the professor using the interactive capability of the Simulation, force the student consultants to reconsider their assumptions, flags, roadmap, and scenarios. The task now becomes one of deciding how much must the basic roadmap be modified. Or more seriously, is the chosen strategy even viable? In other words, change has become, not a possibility, but a reality.

In doing the three assignments, the students are essentially asked to assess the strategic fit between Henzger and Cheroca and to plan a business strategy for the company given the three options and the chaotic situation. To assist them in doing that, the Simulation utilizes a methodology contained in four, cross-toolset forms. Each form compels the students to maintain a running list or explicit agenda of what they are thinking and doing as they "evolve" their strategic plan for Henzger in Cheroca.

The first cumulative form is for *assumptions*. Its use requires explicitly stating what underpins their thinking. As noted in the Simulation, "Emerging economies are characterized by uncertainty, gaps, volatility, and poor or misleading information. They often have cultures, structures, procedures, and legacies which may be subtle and unfamiliar . . . This form encourages users to specify assumptions, evaluate the potential impact if they are incorrect and indicate actions to verify assumed information . . . An important consideration is the cascading effect of assumptions." By detailing the assumptions and asking how they might affect the strategic plan, the student consultants are learning not to take for granted in other countries that which is generally accepted in the United States.

The next cumulative form is for *flags*. Flags "indicate important areas where it is evident there is inadequate information or where specified changes could have significant impact." The impact would be on the resources and capabilities that are part of the strategic plan. Flags can also have a cascading effect, and the issues they raise need to be addressed in the roadmap. For Henzger in Cheroca, the political unrest that could lead to a civil war and divide the country represents a flag that ought to be planned for in terms of possible responses if it does occur.

To assist the students in planning for uncertainties, the designers of the Simulation created a third form–*Scenario Input*. It is free-form in nature and asks the students to "evolve" possible situations or contexts that could come about in Cheroca. The scenarios are developed while the students think through the potential implications of their assumptions and flags. These "will ultimately be prioritized and scenarios will be built considering how 'worlds' would look that richly reflect the essence of these ideas."

The final output or form produced by the students is labeled a *roadmap*. Based on their thinking and planning using the above forms, they then develop an agenda with predicted times and actions for what is necessary to implement the strategy. "Roadmaps indicate task sequence, related resource requirements by time needed and actions to develop or acquire and deploy resources." (The students have produced some very creative and stimulating roadmaps using PowerPoint software.) At its core, the roadmap indicates the strategic action plan recommended by the student consultants to the management of Henzger.

In summary, these four forms together provide a framework for handling the formulation-implementation challenge that lies at the heart of strategy-making. Clearly, any and all classroom endeavors favor formulation over implementation, but the roadmap exercise counters that inherent bias by encouraging the students to put actions with their plans. Additionally, it creates visual images of the uncertainties and chaos often encountered in emerging economies. Thus, it not only makes salient the peculiarities of emerging economies, but it also addresses the challenge found in the formulation-implementation conundrum.

THE STRATEGY CONCEPT AND THE RESOURCE-BASED VIEW

One finding from the three experiments dealt with the business strategy concept and the difficulties the students encountered with it. The difficulty seems to stem from the concept itself and not from a weakness of the students or the Simulation. How can students or the designers of a simulation be expected to exercise the business strategy concept when strategy scholars themselves are still struggling to understand and explain what strategy is?

To illustrate this point, Makadok (2001) takes on one of the most troublesome issues facing strategy scholars. The issue is the debate over which is more important–the resource base or the activity capability–to achieve superior financial returns. He cites Williamson (1991, 76) as evidence for this issue. "The leading efficiency approaches to business strategy are the resource-based and the dynamic capabilities approach . . . It is not obvious to me how these two literatures will play out–either individually or in combination. Plainly, they deal with core issues. Possibly they will be joined." Ghemawat and Pisano (1999, 112) affirmed that "Many researchers in strategic management, when asked to identify the key fault line in strategy today, might cite the tension between the 'activity-system' and 'resource-based' views of the firm. As their names indicate, these two theories embody very different opinions about how strategists ought to think about the structures of firms: in terms of the activities that firms perform versus the resources that firms deploy." Makadok (2001), in his article, did not resolve the debate; instead he moved the field toward a synthesis of the two competing theories.

The author cites this debate to confirm the observation that students using the Simulation struggle with the business strategy concept because the concept itself is fuzzy, difficult, and uncertain. One cannot expect students to master that which the scholars still do not understand. Assuming that the scholarly debate is indeed legitimate, the question then becomes what to do in the emerging economies course? Which theory should be taught given that the design of this course is to teach business strategy for emerging economies and not the debate about business strategy theories? The author has chosen to emphasize resources or the RBV over activities for the reasons noted below.

As already alluded to, the strategy ideas espoused in the emerging economies course should not be divorced from the strategy notions taught in the strategy/policy course that MBA students must take given the AACSB mandate for an integrative experience. To teach strategy in different courses with unrelated ideas and notions seems not only inefficient but also ridiculous. Plus, the uncertainty really confuses and frustrates students. The substance of an emerging economies course provides enough uncertainty for the vast majority of learners. With this admonishment in mind, the choice of the RBV was based on two criteria–what is being taught in the policy/strategy course and what is more consistent with the strategy viewpoint of the Simulation.

First, since the RBV became the dominant strategy theory in the 1990s, it seemed the better choice for the emerging economies course. It would be prominent in strategy/policy textbooks, and the students should be familiar with it. For students who had not yet taken the strategy/policy course, its use in the emerging economies class would be consistent with what they would later see in that course. Second, this author's understanding of the Simulation has persuaded him that it is more resource-based than activity-based. Without a doubt, it does look at activities. However, all its three strategic options require either an alliance with or an acquisition of already existing resources. The options are explained and then judged by the students on their resources more than their activities. Thus, the options are resource-centered, not activity-centered. In light of both these criteria, the choice of the RBV seemed to be the better fit with the Simulation.

The RBV framework chosen by the author for the emerging economies course is the one developed by Collis and Montgomery (1997). Both authors are recognized strategy scholars, and their approach to the RBV seems well documented and balanced. As already stated, balanced means that they do not find it necessary to attack the older, Industry Structure Model and the activity chain with which it is often associated. In fact, they attempt to merge the earlier theory with the RBV. How successful they are in doing that is an open question. The text and case book that Collis and Montgomery have authored includes more than just business strategy. It also covers corporate strategy, and it does an excellent job of linking business and corporate together. Nevertheless, for the emerging economies course the level of concern is the business one, which permits the more abstract topic of corporate strategy to be avoided.

The fundamental idea of the RBV is that firm value or rents are derived from a resource base that has value in the marketplace. The starting point for determining value is to specify what makes up a resource base. For Collis and Montgomery, there are three types of resources–tangible assets, intangible assets, and organizational capabilities. An important consideration from the RBV perspective is that the firm must have these three types of resources at hand or in stock if value is to be earned from them. Tangible assets are goods or items that can be found on the balance sheet. Thus, a factory that can package baby food or an orchard that can provide fruit would be a tangible asset for Henzger. Intangible assets are more abstract but equally as important as tangible assets. Brand names, patents, and relationships are classes of intangibles that matter in many industries. For Henzger in Cheroca, an alliance with an established company that already has a known brand and ties to the government would give Henzger immediate access to important intangible assets. In addition to having the assets, a firm must also be able to utilize them productively through its capabilities, its processes and people. Organizational capabilities represent the crux of the RBV as a theory and also the debate between strategy scholars noted above. In reference to capabilities, assets that cannot be utilized, i.e., jars of baby food that fail to reach the store shelves efficiently and timely, will not result in economic rents for the firm.

In order for the assets and capabilities of the resource base created by Henzger's choice of a strategic option to have value, three criteria must be met simultaneously:

1. Demand. The product or service must satisfy the customer's need at an acceptable price. Is the baby food priced right in Cheroca? In light of changes in customer needs, the firm has to be capable of adapting so that it can continue to satisfy the dynamics of customer demand.
2. Scarcity. The resource base must not be readily available; it needs to be in short supply. Are there readily available substitutes for baby food in Cheroca? It should provide a distinctive competence that sustains a competitive advantage. It will be valuable if it is inimitable, i.e., others cannot easily duplicate it.
3. Appropriability. The profits earned from the resource base must be captured by the owner of that base. Can Henzger readily repatriate profits to the United States? Demand and scarcity create little value if the rents from the resources are not capable of being captured.

The important consideration for students to remember when evaluating a resource base is that the three criteria must be satisfied jointly, i.e., the combination of assets and capabilities in the chosen strategic option must manifest demand, scarcity, and appropriability for Henzger in Cheroca.

To make this point clearer about baby food, one needs only to examine Collis and Montgomery's highlighted presentation of Gerber Products Company and its enviable position in the U.S. market (1997, 29).

> Few firms can boast the kind of brand recognition and loyalty enjoyed . . . Generations of American parents, themselves raised on Gerber baby food, wouldn't buy anything else. The firm has a 65-year history and commands more than 70 percent of the U.S. baby food market. When Gerber was acquired by Sandoz Ltd., a

> Swiss pharmaceutical firm, in 1994, its tangible net worth, including its plants and inventory, was less than $300 million. One might wonder why Sandoz was willing to pay $3.7 billion for the firm . . . The answer lies in Gerber's intangible assets: its brand name, reputation, and considerable expanse of supermarket shelf space. These are the assets Gerber's competitors have vied for decades to imitate, with little success.

Two of the criteria, demand and scarcity, are being met in Gerber's favor, but appropriability, though not mentioned by Collis and Montgomery, could become unfavorable if the supermarkets were to demand a larger share of the selling price. To sustain its competitive advantage in the U.S., Gerber under Sandoz must maintain all three criteria in its favor.

The above points provide an overview of Collis and Montgomery's RBV framework, which, as already noted, was chosen because of its balanced approach to the strategy concept. Additional analytical details and a link to the Industry Structure Model are also provided by them, but all that is secondary to the core idea that resources, assets and capabilities, have value when they satisfy the three criteria. As demonstrated above, that core idea can be intertwined with the Simulation and thereby give the students in the emerging economies course a more coherent and parsimonious view of knowledge about the business strategy concept.

SUMMARY AND FINAL COMMENTS

In terms of the Emerging Economies Course Triangle, the findings of the three experiments, which prompted the utilization of the Simulation and the RBV, indicated that attention to the substance of each side is necessary in an emerging economies course. Side a, *general and specific information about the particulars of emerging economies*, should be presented with ample depth and breadth so that the students can appreciate the often unique reality of an emerging economy. Side b, *knowledge about the business strategy concept*, can be based on the RBV and reduce much of the confusion inherent to the strategy notion. This, of course, assumes that the RBV will continue as the dominant strategy paradigm. Side c, *an integrative experience*, ought to be rooted in the Simulation due to its conceptual overlap with the RBV. The Simulation permits the students to enjoy and benefit from a learning experience that is pedagogically consistent and conceptually sound. As presented and discussed in this article, there is an affinity between the substances represented by sides b and c that compliments and reinforces the purpose of the emerging economies course and the overall curriculum design of a business school.

More specifically, the linkages between the RBV and the Simulation in an emerging economy become more visible as the students endeavor to analyze the three strategic options contained in the latter. Each option when hypothetically coupled with the resource base of Henzger permits the analyst to examine how that strategy will be helped or hindered as the tangible and intangible assets plus the organizational capabilities of each Cherocan business are supplemented by the assets and capabilities of Henzger. The durability of the possible strategies can then be studied from the perspective of the many uncertainties that abound in Cheroca. In doing this, the students must formulate roadmaps–visible representations–of how their selected strategies will cope with these potential problems, i.e., how RBV thinking will handle a strategic setting where the contextual stability of the developed world does not exist.

The author believes that a final comment is in order regarding the Simulation and its use. First, the experiments do not demonstrate definitively that it is a superior teaching tool. As revealed by Oviatt, Bansal, and Houghton (2000), computer-aided technologies may enhance student learning about the technology but not about the substance of the course. The technology clearly has appeal to the students, but its efficacy in their learning is still a question needing an answer. Second, the Simulation is in English and its tools rely upon that language and very specific/special terms for accomplishing their purpose. Those terms must be mastered by the students to use the Simulation well. A native speaker of English can master the terminology without much trouble; however, for the user who is not fluent in English the terms become a challenge if not an obstacle. Until it is translated into other languages, this presents a real burden for those of us who desire to utilize the Simulation with students who reside in the world of real emerging economies and with the intent of assisting those economies in their development.

REFERENCES

Collis, D.J. and Montgomery, C.A. (1997). *Corporate Strategy: Resources and the Scope of the Firm.* Irwin, Chicago.

Ghemawat, P. and Pisano, G. (1999). Building and Sustaining Success, in *Strategy and the Business Landscape*, by Ghemawat, P. Addison-Wesley, Reading.

Gilbert, D.R. (1992). *The Twilight of Corporate Strategy: A Comparative Ethical Critique*, Oxford University Press, New York.

Jenkins, J.R.G. (1998). The Role of Simulations in International Management Education, *Journal of Teaching in International Business*, Vol. 9, No. 3, pp. 43-58.

Kaynak, E. and Kucukemiroglu, O. (1997). Program and Curriculum Development in International Marketing in an Emerging Economy: Issues and Strategies, *Journal of Teaching in International Business*, Vol. 9, No. 1, pp. 51-63.

Makadok, R. (2001). Toward a Synthesis of the Resource-Based and Dynamic-Capability Views of Rent Creation, *Strategic Management Journal*, Vol. 22, No. 5, pp. 387-401.

McGraw, P. and Palmer, Ian. (1999). A Structured Debriefing Process for International Business Culture Simulations, *Journal of Teaching in International Business*, Vol. 11, No. 2, pp. 39-51.

Mintzberg, H. (1995). *The Rise and Fall of Strategic Planning*, The Free Press, New York.

Oviatt, B.M., Bansal, P., and Houghton, S. (2000). An Experimental Test of CD-ROM Aided Instruction in Transnational Management, *Journal of Teaching in International Business*, Vol. 11, No. 3, pp. 37-47.

Ruhe, J.A. and Allen, W.R. (2001). NEWS Ltd.: Simulations for Trust Development, *Journal of Teaching in International Business*, Vol. 12, No. 4, pp. 29-43.

Williamson, O.E. (1991). Strategizing, Economizing, and Economic Organization, *Strategic Management Journal*, Winter Special Issue, 75-94.

Wolfe, J. (1993). A Forecast of Business Gaming in the Year 2010, *Simulation & Gaming*, Vol. 24, No. 3, pp. 381-383.

Using Internet Resources in Teaching Financial Reporting and Analysis of Multinational Enterprises

Abdel M. Agami

SUMMARY. There has been an increase in the number and type of sources of corporate financial information on the Internet in recent years. The number of corporations that have web pages which post corporate financial information is increasing; in addition, many government and regulatory agencies are also posting corporate financial information. Furthermore, there are some third-party sites that post corporate financial information. In recent years some software has been developed or is in the process of being developed to gather, analyze, and monitor information available on the Internet to accomplish specific tasks on behalf of users. The purpose of this article is to provide some sources of corporate financial information on the Internet and illustrate how to use these resources in teaching international business and, more specifically, financial reporting and analysis of multinational enterprises and to point out some of the advantages and limitations of these resources. *[Article copies available for a fee from The Haworth Document Delivery Service: 1-800-HAWORTH. E-mail address: <getinfo@haworthpressinc.com> Website: <http://www.HaworthPress.com> © 2003 by The Haworth Press, Inc. All rights reserved.]*

Abdel M. Agami is affiliated with the Accounting Department, College of Business and Public Administration, Old Dominion University, Norfolk, VA 23529 (E-mail: aagami@odu.edu).

[Haworth co-indexing entry note]: "Using Internet Resources in Teaching Financial Reporting and Analysis of Multinational Enterprises." Agami, Abdel M. Co-published simultaneously in *Journal of Teaching in International Business* (International Business Press, an imprint of The Haworth Press, Inc.) Vol. 14, No. 2/3, 2003, pp. 115-131; and: *Digital Technology in Teaching International Business* (ed: Lloyd C. Russow) International Business Press, an imprint of The Haworth Press, Inc., 2003, pp. 115-131. Single or multiple copies of this article are available for a fee from The Haworth Document Delivery Service [1-800-HAWORTH 9:00 a.m. - 5:00 p.m. (EST). E-mail address: getinfo@haworthpressinc.com].

KEYWORDS. Financial information, Internet, software, resources, teaching, financial reporting, analysis, multinational enterprises

There has been a dramatic increase in the number and type of sources of corporate financial information on the Internet in recent years. The number of corporations having web pages that post corporate financial information is increasing; in addition, many governments and regulatory agencies such as the US Securities and Exchange Commission (SEC), Canadian System for Electronic Document Analysis and Retrieval (SEDAR), the German Neuer Market Exchange, the French Commission des Operations de Bourse, the Amsterdam Stock Exchange, the Rio de Janeiro Stock Exchange, and many others are also posting corporate financial information. Furthermore, there are some third-party sites that post corporate financial information, a few of which are Yahoo!, Hoover, MSN Money Central, Zacks Investment Research, Inc., Thomson Investor Network, and Corporate Window. In recent years, some software has been developed or is in the process of being developed to gather, analyze, and monitor information available on the Internet in order to accomplish specific tasks on behalf of users. These software programs are known as Intelligent Internet Agents (IIAs). While IIAs have a broad variety of purposes and uses, some of them, such as "FRAANK" and "WARREN," can be used for financial reporting and analysis of multinational enterprises. The number of IIAs available today is, unfortunately, small; according to some users, they are not very reliable and lack privacy. The purpose of this article is to provide some sources of corporate financial information on the Internet and illustrate how to use these resources in teaching international business and, more specifically, financial reporting and analysis of multinational enterprises and to point out some of the advantages and limitations of these resources.

FINANCIAL REPORTING AND ANALYSIS OF MULTINATIONAL ENTERPRISES

As a result of the increase in competition, decrease in cost of transportation, improved means of communication and the revolution in information technology, many US companies have extended their operations outside the US and many foreign companies are doing business in the United States. Today companies acquire their resources such as material, labor, and capital wherever they are cheap and/or of high quality, and market their products and services wherever there is a demand for them. Multinational enterprises (MNEs) face unique problems that are different from companies that operate in only one country. MNEs raise their capital needs globally to minimize their cost of capital. They also procure resources from various countries to minimize cost and/or to increase the quality of these resources, locate their factories wherever the cost of labor is relatively cheap, and market their products and services wherever they can maximize their revenues. As a result, many of these MNEs have to comply with the laws, regulations, and standards of each country in which they operate. Another serious problem they face is exposure to foreign exchange risk, political risk, and the need to adapt to different cultures and languages. These variables complicate the financial reporting and analysis of those MNEs.

Because financial reporting and analysis of MNEs is complicated by the factors mentioned above, there has been a steady increase in the number of business schools offering courses that deal with the financial reporting and analysis of MNEs. Some of the issues covered in such courses include: (1) corporate financial reporting in global capital markets; (2) intercompany equity investment and cross-border mergers and acquisitions; (3) measuring and reporting of gains or losses resulting from foreign exchange transaction, hedging, and reporting currency; (4) segmental and geographical reporting; (5) financial analysis of MNEs; and (6) reporting the impact of MNEs on environment and employment.

The method used in teaching this course usually includes lecture and discussion. The course also uses the case method, which is a very effective means of bringing to students' attention the complex issues that face MNEs in real life. In addition to simulating real world situations, the case method arouses students' interest and generates more student participation and interaction. An independent project is usually assigned to each student or a teams of students. The projects involve issues faced by MNEs and require students to play the roles of CEO, banker, financial analyst, auditor, and/or stockholders. In their pursuit for solutions to the problems, students have to gather information about the company from many sources including the Internet, analyze this information, interpret it, and make decisions to resolve the issues facing the MNE [Agami, 1983; Foroughi & Reed, 1987; Sherman, 1987; Stout & Schweikart, 1989; Agami, 1991; Huang & Mintz, 1992; Adams & Roberts, 1994; Tondkar et al., 1998; and Lainez & Callao, 2000].

SOURCES OF CORPORATE FINANCIAL INFORMATION

Corporate financial information such as financial statements, footnotes, auditors' reports, stock prices, and other related information can be obtained from different sources. A hard copy or a microfiche copy of many companies' reports are available in school libraries, or can be obtained directly from corporations or local brokers. They are also available in summary form along with financial analysis through financial services published by Standard & Poor's, Moody's, Bradstreet, and other publishers of financial information, which are also available in many school libraries. Compact D SEC and Compact D WORLDSCOPE are two databases that provide a directory and detailed financial information for publicly held companies and may also be available at a local university library. Compact D SEC includes records for over 12,000 US companies filing with the SEC. Compact D WORLDSCOPE includes over 15,000 foreign companies [Agami, 1993].

Today there is a wealth of financial information about US and foreign corporations available on the Internet. This information is posted on the Internet by companies on their web pages; it can also be obtained from the web sites of regulatory agencies such as the US SEC and foreign security and exchange regulators; also many private third-party organizations such as brokers, financial analysts and big CPA firms make such information available in their sites.

Some of the sources report the information as posted by companies; others put it in summary form along with analysis, comments, and/or recommendations.

Companies' Web Sites

Most companies, especially the large ones, have web sites and most of these sites contain a section titled "Investor Relations." A survey of the largest 30 companies in 22 countries found that 100% of the top companies in Australia, Canada, France, Germany, Sweden, and the US have web sites. The countries on the bottom of the list were Malaysia (43%) and Chile (53%). However, not every company that has a web site reported financial information. The Investor Relations section posted financial information about the company such as quarterly and annual financial statements, financial history of the company, SEC filings such as 10-K and 10-Q, stock quotes, press releases, and other related financial information [Lymer et al., 1999]. However, the information reported by corporations varied from one company to another. Some companies include presentations they made to analysts, earnings commentary, investor relations calendar of events, web sites that have published articles about them, etc. In some web sites, the companies offer several media for downloading this information, such as word processing, spreadsheet, PDF, etc. Recently the American Institute of Certified Public Accountants (AICPA), with support from six information technology companies, the five largest accounting firms, and other organizations initiated a project to develop a more sophisticated language for financial reporting known as Extensible Business Reporting Language (XBML). The purpose of this project is to provide a standard-based framework that allows for more efficient preparation and use of the financial information reported by companies [FASB, 2000]. In a survey conducted by the Association for Investment Management and Research (AIMR) of 2000 financial analysts and portfolio managers, 65% of the 355 respondents noted that easy access to corporate information by way of a corporate web site makes it easier for them to analyze companies [AIMR, 1999]. There are a number of organizations that evaluate the quality and rank the Investor Relations section of companies' web sites such as Bulletin Board Room, Inc. <www.off-on.com>, the Motley Fool <www.fool.com>, Dow Jones Business Directory <bd.dowjones.com>, and Browne Internet Solutions <www.investor-rel.com>. A good way of getting to the web sites of US and international companies is the Report Gallery <http://www.reportgallery.com>. Report Gallery, Hoover's, Forbes, and Fortune are the most complete and up-to-date listing of annual reports and related financial reports online. For example, the Report Gallery currently lists over 2,200 annual reports and covers the Fortune 500 companies and has a special site for international companies <http://www.reportgallery.com/International.htm>.

Government and Regulatory Agencies

Government (federal, state, and local) as well as regulatory agencies such as the SEC, FTC, New York Stock Exchange, NASDAQ, Federal Reserve Board, American Stock Exchange, and Chicago Mercantile Exchange provide up-to-date information on the stocks traded at a particular exchange and/or the financial information filed with them. While the information posted on these sites tends to be formal and lacks the format users like due to legal requirements stipulated by these agencies, the information is usually of a higher degree of reliability than those reported on the companies' sites. Appendix A provides the web site addresses of some regulatory bodies in the United States.

Many regulatory agencies in foreign countries have followed the US example. For example, the System for Electronic Document Analysis and Retrieval (SEDAR) in Canada publishes corporate filings on the web. The Australian Securities and Investment Commission (ASIC) encourages companies to file financial information electronically. A system of electronic filing is planned by the Austrian Firmenbuch. In the UK there are also plans to introduce electronic filing. Companies listed on the German Neuer Market Stock Exchange can now list their financial information on the Exchange's web site. In France the Commission des Opérations de Bourse (COB) has regulated the filing of financial information electronically by French companies. Appendix A provides the web site addresses of some foreign regulatory agencies [Lymer et al., 1999].

Third Party Sites

The number of third-party sites that post financial information about companies has been increasing tremendously in the last three years. Some of the information posted on these sites includes companies' financial statements, SEC filings, companies' press releases, and stock quotes. Many of these sites include enhanced search, downloading, and formatting choices. Some of the sites provide analysis of financial statements, earnings-per-share information, analysts' reports, and other useful information. Examples of third-party sites are: Edgar Online; FreeEdgar; Media General Financial Services, Inc.; DigiTrade; Daily Stock.com; Investor Relations Information Network; Quote.com; Yahoo! Finance; etc. Appendix B provides the web site addresses of some third parties.

Intelligent Internet Agents (IIAs)

An IIA may be defined as a software and/or hardware that is programmed to perform a number of defined tasks on behalf of users. IIAs have three important properties: autonomy, learning, and cooperation. Autonomy means that the IIAs are able to operate without the need of interference from humans; IIAs are able to learn as they interact with the environment, humans, and each other; and IIAs are able to cooperate with other agents and humans [Woodridge & Jennings, 1995; Nwana & Ndumu, 1996; Franklin & Graessner, 1997; Kogan et al., 1998; and Baldwin & Williams, 1999].

IIAs can be utilized in gathering and analyzing information from different sources on the Internet. IIAs could also update the information gathered and analyze it periodically or when new information becomes available [Baldwin & Williams, 1999].

Non-Financial IIAs

A number of IIAs have been developed recently. One IIA assists in locating the homepage of individuals on the web; another scans new articles located on the web; another locates a given book and its price; another looks for web pages related to employment opportunities; another searches the Internet for desired music tastes; one searches for bargains; etc. Appendix C shows some of these IIAs, their functions, and their Internet addresses [Baldwin & Williams, 1999].

Financial IIAs

There are at least three IIAs that can be used in analyzing financial information related to corporations: FRAANK; WARREN; and EDGARScan. FRAANK was developed jointly by researchers from Rutgers University and the University of Kansas. FRAANK includes: (1) an EDGAR Agent which searches the EDGAR database for a 10-Q report of any company that is required to file with the SEC, lists the key accounting items, and calculates financial ratios; and (2) a Stock Agent which brings back the current stock information from the quote.com database.

WARREN was developed by Carnegie Mellon University and named for the American investor and author Warren Buffet. It is an IIA for financial portfolio management over time using the information resources available over the Internet. It interacts with users, receives user input, and displays results. It helps users perform tasks, formulates problem-solving plans, and carries out these plans by coordinating and exchanging information with other software agents. It provides intelligent access to a heterogeneous collection of information sources. It also helps to match agents requesting services with agents that provide those services.

EDGARScan is a state-of-the-art technology for parsing the key financial data detailed in the SEC documents filed by every public company. EDGARScan automatically locates all of the key financial tables and normalizes the data into a common format that is comparable across companies. The "Benchmarking Assistant" performs graphical benchmarking interactively. Tables showing company comparisons can be downloaded as Excel charts. Appendix D lists the functions and the web addresses of FRAANK, WARREN, and EDGARScan.

ILLUSTRATING HOW TO INTEGRATE INTERNET RESOURCES IN TEACHING FINANCIAL REPORTING AND ANALYSIS OF MNES

In this section, the author provides an illustration of how to integrate Internet resources in teaching financial reporting and analysis of DaimlerChrysler AG (the company that resulted from the merger of Daimler-Benz AG and Chrysler Corporation). Daimler-Benz AG Case is one of the cases in *Corporate Financial Reporting and Analysis* [Hawkins, 1998], the text used by the author. The case was published in 1993 to illustrate the issues and problems faced by US investors in analyzing a foreign company that is listed on a US stock exchange (NYSE). The objectives of the case are to: (1) portray to students problems such as variations in accounting standards in different countries, differences in format of presenting financial information from one country to another, different terminology, differences in disclosure level, tax code, legal environment, cultures, and the use of different currencies for measurement and exchanges; and (2) show how investors overcome such problems.

The case also provides very valuable information as to how Daimler-Benz got started, when automobiles were invented, and how Daimler-Benz grew over time from a two-man company to one of the most prestigious auto companies in the world. It also provides insight into how difficult it is for global companies to raise capital globally. As of 1993, the company used German accounting standards for financial reporting. In compliance with the SEC requirements, the company had to adjust its income and equity for the differences between German accounting standards and US accounting standards. The case includes Summary Financial Data for the years ending December 31, 1988 to 1992 and reconciliation of income and equity from German to US accounting standards.

While the information in the case is very significant for a course that deals with financial reporting and analysis of MNEs, there are several significant events that happened to Daimler-Benz subsequent to 1992. On September 17, 1993 Daimler-Benz published US GAAP-based financial data for the first time. On the same day, Daimler-Benz American Depository Shares were approved for listing on the New York Stock Exchange. On May 17, 1998 Daimler-Benz AG and Chrysler Corporation announced their plans to merge. On July 23, 1998 the merger plan was approved by the European Union. On July 31, 1998 the merger was approved by the US Federal Trade Commission. On September 18, 1998 the merger was approved by Chrysler Corporation and Daimler-Benz AG shareholders, and the stock of the new company DaimlerChrysler began trading under the symbol DCX. The author asks students to utilize sources available on the Internet to obtain information about events that affected the company subsequent to the date of publication of the case. Appendix D presents some illustrations of Internet sources that update the information in the DaimlerChrysler case. Some of these sources provide some numbers and statistics related to the demand and supply on autos globally; some provide history and background information about Daimler-Benz AG and Chrysler Corporation; some sources provide articles written about events that occurred subsequent to the date of publication of the case that affected both companies; some sources provide financial statements, annual reports, 10-K, and other related financial information published about the companies subsequent to the date of the publication of the case; some of these sources provide information and charts related to the stock movement of the company; and, finally, sources for other cases written about the company that deal with other issues.

In the instructor's opinion, these sources increase student interest in the discussion of the case, make the case alive, and help students develop their research skills to find information related to specific problems and cases dealt with in the class and problems they may encounter in the future in their careers and endeavors. This also helps provide students with up-to-date information and supplements a serious problem that published sources suffer from, namely being out-of-date by the time they are published.

EVALUATION OF INTERNET SOURCES

The Internet makes financial information available to all users at no cost or at a very low cost, increases the speed of its dissemination, and eases use of the information. Today, any investor with a computer and a modem can access financial information related to practically any public company in the world. In the past such privilege was reserved for only an elite of professional investment analysts. The SEC recognizes that the use of electronic media enhances the efficiency of the securities markets by allowing for the rapid dissemination of information to investors and financial markets in a more cost-efficient, widespread, and equitable manner than traditional-based methods [SEC, 1999].

On the other hand, some studies have indicated that Internet information might be sometimes lacking in its completeness and consistency. In one case an "annual report" link on one company's web site led to the president's letter, and the balance of the report was not included on the web site. In a second case, a company's hard copy annual report contained a detailed index, but the report produced on the web site did not. In a third case, financial statements were summarized into standard form that omitted many details, footnotes and auditors' report; this reduced the usefulness and reliability of the information [FASB, 2000].

SUMMARY AND CONCLUSIONS

This article has illustrated some of the sources available on the Internet for extracting corporate financial information and how to use these sources in teaching financial reporting and analysis of multinational enterprises. This information includes companies' web sites, government and regulatory agencies sites, third party sites, and Intelligent Internet Agents.

The use of financial information available on the Internet enriches the discussion in class and provides up-to-date information relevant to the issues discussed in the course. Information available on the Internet is frequently available at no cost or at a very low cost; the Internet increases the speed of dissemination of the information; it makes the use of information easier; and it provides the information on a timely basis. On the other hand, the information on the Internet sometimes lacks completeness; it is not readily comparable from one company to another; in many cases it is not prepared by experts (such as accountants); in some cases the information is not prepared according to generally accepted accounting principles; and it is not always audited by a certified public accountant. Other sources should be used to supplement Internet sources whenever it is possible.

In summary, the use of Internet sources of corporate information in the financial reporting and analysis of multinational enterprises adds value to the course. It helps students develop their research skills to find up-to-date information related to specific problems and cases dealt with in the course and problems they may encounter in the future in their chosen careers and endeavors. It also supplements or remedies the lack of up-to-date information in textbooks and other educational materials due to the time lag needed for publication.

REFERENCES

AIMR. *Using Technology and the Internet: Researching Corporate Strategic and Financial Information.* New York: Association for Investment Management and Research, 1999. <http://www.aimr.com/infocentral/news/99releases/int-study.html>

Adams, C.A., and C.B. Roberts, "International Accounting Education in the UK." *Accounting Education* (Vol. 3, No., 2, 1994), 167-181.

Agami, Abdel M., "The International Accounting Course: State of the Art." *Journal of Accounting Education* (Fall 1983), 67-77.

Agami, Abdel M., "Adding International Dimension to the Accounting Curriculum." *Journal of Teaching in International Business* (Vol. 3, No. 2, 1991), 53-63.

Agami, Abdel M., "Using International Financial Databases in Teaching International Accounting Courses." *Journal of Teaching in International Business* (Vol. 4, No. 3/4, 1993), 103-113.

Agami, Abdel, "Developing Comparable Accounting Information for Global Capital Markets." In *Selected International Investment Portfolio*, edited by James C. Barker. New York: Elsevier Science, Inc., 1998, 3-12.

Baldwin, A., and S. Williams, "The Future of Intelligent Internet Agents in European Financial Reporting." *The European Accounting Review* (Vol. 8, No. 2, 1999), 303-319.

FASB. *Electronic Reporting Research Project.* Norwalk, CT: FASB, 2000. Also available on the FASB web site at <http://www.fasb.org>.

Foroughi, Tahirih, and Barbara Reed, "A Survey of the Present and Desirable International Accounting Topics in Accounting Education." *International Journal of Accounting* (Fall 1987), 69-82.

Franklin, S., and A. Grassner, "Is It an Agent, or Just a Program?" In *Intelligent Agents III*, edited by J.P. Muller et al. Berlin: Springer-Verlag, 1997, 21-36.

Hawkins, F. David. *Corporate Financial Reporting and Analysis: Text and Cases.* New York: Irwin/McGraw-Hill, 1998, 887-908.

Huang, Jiunn C., and Steven M. Mintz, "International Accounting Education: A Global Perspective." *The Accounting Educators' Journal* (Vol. IV, No. 1, 1992), 69-85.

Kogan, A. et al., "FRAANK: Financial Reporting and Auditing Agent with Net Knowledge." *Collected Abstracts of the American Accounting Association Annual Meeting 1998*, 49.

Lainez, José, and Susane Callao, "The Effect of Accounting Diversity on International Financial Analysis: Empirical Evidence." *The International Journal of Accounting* (Vol. 35, No. 1, 2000), 65-83.

Lamier, J., "Intelligent agents = stupid human?" <http://www.hotwired.com/braintennis>.

Lymer et al. *Business Reporting on the Internet*. London: IASC, 1999.

Nwana, H., and Ndumu, D., "An Introduction to Agent Technology." *BT Technology Journal* (Vol. 14, No. 4, 1996), 55-67.

Securities and Exchange Commission. *Current Issues and Rulemaking Project*. January 21, 1999.

Sherman, W. Richard, "Internationalizing the Accounting Curriculum." *Journal of Accounting Education* (Fall 1987), 259-275.

Stout, David E., and James A. Schweikart, "The Relevance of International Accounting to the Accounting Curriculum: A Comparison of Practitioner and Educator Opinion." *Issues in Accounting Education* (Spring 1989), 126-143.

Tondkar, R.H., M.A. Flanigan, A. Adhikari, J.A. Hora, "Internationalizing Accounting Education Through an Integration Approach: A Survey of US Schools." *International Journal of Accounting* (Vol. 33, No. 4, 1998), 483-507.

Woodridge, M., and N. Jennings, "Intelligent Agent: Theory and Practice." *Knowledge Engineering Review* (Vol. 10, No. 2, 1995), 115-152.

APPENDIX A

Some US Government and Regulatory Agency Sites

Site Name	Internet Address
American Stock Exchange	http://www.amex.com/
Chicago Board of Trade	http://www.cbot.com/
Chicago Board Options Exchange	http://www.cboe.com/
Chicago Mercantile Exchange	http://www.cme.com/
Federal Reserve Board: Board of Governors	http://www.bog.frb.fed.us/
General Accounting Office of the USA	http://www.gao.gov/
NASDAQ	http://www.nasdaq.com/
New York Stock Exchange	http://www.nyse.com/
Securities and Exchange Commission	http://www.sec.gov/
Canadian firms	http://strategis.ic.gc.ca/sc_coinf/engdoc/homepac.html
Neuer Market Stock Exchange of Germany	http://www.neuer-markt.de
The French Commission des Opérations de Bourse (COB)	http://www.cob.fr/wCOB
The Amsterdam Stock Exchange	http://www.econ.vu.n/englis/home.html
The Rio de Janeiro Stock Exchange	http://www.embratel.net.br/infoserv/bvvg

Source: Lymer et al. *Business Reporting on the Internet.* London: IASC, 1999.

APPENDIX B

Some Third-Party Sites

Site Name	Internet Address
Edgar Online	http://www.edgar-online.com
FreeEdgar	http://www.freeedgar.com
Media General Financial Services, Inc.	http://www.mgfs.com
DigiTrade	http://www.digitrade.com
Daily Stocks.com	http://www.dailystocks.com
Investor Relations Information Network	http://www.irin.com
Quote.com	http://www.quote.com
Yahoo! Finance	http://www.yahoo.com
Corporate Window	http://www.corporatewindow.com
Hoover's Online Business Network	http://www.hoovers.com
MSN Money Central	http://www.msn.com
The Public Register	http://www.prars.com
Web 100	http://www.w100.com
Zacks Investment Research, Inc.	http://www.zacks.com
Thomason Investor Network	http://www.thomsoninvest.com
10K Wizard	http://www.tenkwizard.com
Standard & Poor's	http://www.standardpoor.com

Source: Financial Accounting Standards Board. *Electronic Reporting Research Project.* Norwalk, CT: FASB, 2000.

APPENDIX C

Financial and Non-Financial Intelligent Internet Agencies (IIAs)

Site Name	Functions	Internet Address
Ahoy	Assists in locating the homepage of individuals on the web	http://ahoy.cs.washington.edu:6060
Smart News Reader	Scans new articles located on the web	http://www.intel.com/newsread.htm
Book Worms Bargainbot	Locates a given book and its price	http://www.ece.curtin.edu au/~saound/bargainbot/
Resume Robot	Looks for web pages containing employment	http://www.onramp.net
Similarities Engine	Searches the Internet for desired music tastes	http://www.ari.com
Bargain Finder	Searches for bargains	http://bf.cstar.accom/bf/
FRAANK	It includes: (1) EDGAR agent that searches the EDGAR database for a 10-Q report of the company you specify, lists the key accounting items, and calculates the financial ratios; (2) Stock Agent that retrieves the current stock information from quote.com database	http://lark.cc.ukans.edu/cgiwrap/sirvasta/agent.cgi
WARREN	It helps users monitor financial portfolio management over time using information resources available over the Internet. It interacts with users, receives users' input, and displays results. It helps users perform tasks, formulate problem-solving plans, and carry out these plans.	http://www.cs.cmu.edu/~softagent/warren/
EDGARScan	EDGARScan is a state-of-the-art technology for parsing the key financial data detailed in the SEC documents filed by every public company. EDGARScan automatically locates all of the key financial tables and normalizes the data into a common format that is comparable across companies. The "Benchmarking Assistant" performs graphical benchmarking interactively. Tables showing company comparisons can be downloaded as Excel charts.	http://www.edgarscan.com/

Source: Baldwin, A., and W. Williams, "The Future of Intelligent Internet Agents in European Financial Reporting." The European Accounting Review (Vol. 8, No. 2, 1999), 303-319.

APPENDIX D

Illustration of Internet Sources that Update Information in the DaimlerChrysler AG Case

INFORMATION	INTERNET SOURCE
Statistics about the auto industry	• US Department of Commerce-STAT-USA/Internet http://www.stat-usa.gov • The Alliance of Automobile Manufacturers http://www.autoalliance.org • Autofacts–Pricewaterhousecoopers http://www.autofacts.com • Automotive News http://www.autonews.com • Automotive News International http://www.autonewsinternational.com • Autoweek http://www.autoweek.com • Media General Financial Services http://www.mgfs.com • Automotive News Data Center http://63.236.108.16/datacenter.cms • Investor Guide http://www.investorguide.com
History of Chrysler and Daimler-Benz	• DaimlerChrysler AG http://www.daimlerchrysler.com/history • Hoover's Online: The Business Network http://www.hoovers.com • Investor Guide http://www.investorguide.com
Events subsequent to the date of the case	• Detroit News http://www.detnews.com • BBC News http://news.bbc.co.uk • LEXIS-NEXIS http://web.lexis-nexis.com • Wilson Web http://vweb.hwwilsonweb.com

APPENDIX D (continued)

INFORMATION	INTERNET SOURCE
	• Wall Street Journal http://interactive.wsj.com • New York Times http://www.nytimes.com • CNN http://www.cnn.com • DaimlerChrysler AG http://www.daimlerchrysler.com/merger • Investor Guide http://www.investorguide.com
Financial Statements, Annual Reports, 10-K, and other financial information subsequent to the date of the case publication	• DaimlerChrysler AG http://www.daimlerchrysler.com/investor • US Securities and Exchange Commission http://www.sec.gov • New York Stock Exchange http://www.nyse.com • Yahoo! Finance http://finance.yahoo.com • Corporate Window http://www.corporatewindow.com • Hoover's http://www.hoovers.com • The Public Register's Annual Report Service (PRARS) http://www.prars.com • Big Business on the Web (Web 100) http://metamoney.com • 10-K Wizards http://www.tenkwizard.com • Standard & Poor's http://www.standardpoor.com • EDGARScan http://edgarscan.com • EDGAROnline http://www.edgar-online.com • Investor Guide http://www.investorguide.com

INFORMATION	INTERNET SOURCE
	• Zacks.Com http://my.zacks.com • The Investor Relations Information Network (IRIN) http://www.irin.com
Stock prices	• Yahoo! Finance http://finance.yahoo.com • Corporate Window http://www.corporatewindow.com • Hoover's http://www.quotes.hoovers.com • MSN.COM http://moneycentral.msc.com • The Public Register's Annual Report Service (PRARS) http://www.prars.com/ • EDGAROnline http://www.edgar-online.com • Dividend Discount Model Worksheet http://dividenddiscountmodel.com • Investor Guide http://www.investorguide.com • BigCharts http://stockcharts.com • StockCharts http://stockcharts.com • Zacks.com http://my.zacks.com • QUOTE.COM http://finance.lycos.com
Cases about Chrysler/Daimler: • Mercedez-Benz in Alabama: Lessons from the field, Case No. 9-199-028; Date: November 4, 1998 • Mercedez-Benz, Case No. 9-394-084; Date: November 30, 1993	• Harvard Business School http://www.hbsp.harvard.edu

Adapting to the Online Teaching Environment: Using Literature to Develop Experiential Exercises for International Management

Cathy A. Rusinko

SUMMARY. This paper proposes that literature (e.g., short stories, folktales, etc.) may be a valuable tool in helping to adapt teaching methods to the online environment, particularly in the case of developing experiential exercises that are compatible with either synchronous or asynchronous online learning. In addition, literature can help students to become better international managers, and builds skills valued by curriculum experts and future employers, including communication skills, team building skills, and contextual understanding of cultural diversity issues. The paper includes an example of how to use the folk tale "Stone Soup" to develop an introductory exercise for an international management class. *[Article copies available for a fee from The Haworth Document Delivery Service: 1-800-HAWORTH. E-mail address: <getinfo@haworthpress.com> Website: <http://www.HaworthPress.com> © 2003 by The Haworth Press, Inc. All rights reserved.]*

Cathy A. Rusinko is Assistant Professor of Management, School of Business Administration, Philadelphia University, School House Lane & Henry Avenue, Philadelphia, PA 19144-5497 (E-mail: RusinkoC@PhilaU.edu).

[Haworth co-indexing entry note]: "Adapting to the Online Teaching Environment: Using Literature to Develop Experiential Exercises for International Management." Rusinko, Cathy A. Co-published simultaneously in *Journal of Teaching in International Business* (International Business Press, an imprint of The Haworth Press, Inc.) Vol. 14, No. 2/3, 2003, pp. 133-145; and: *Digital Technology in Teaching International Business* (ed: Lloyd C. Russow) International Business Press, an imprint of The Haworth Press, Inc., 2003, pp. 133-145. Single or multiple copies of this article are available for a fee from The Haworth Document Delivery Service [1-800-HAWORTH 9:00 a.m. - 5:00 p.m. (EST). E-mail address: getinfo@haworthpress.com].

KEYWORDS. Teaching online, experiential exercises, curriculum, literature

INTRODUCTION AND LITERATURE REVIEW

Online learning has enabled tremendous educational potential by allowing learning communities to expand far beyond their traditional boundaries of the classroom, or university, or workplace, or region, or nation (e.g., Shrivastava, 1999). However, in order to tap this tremendous potential successfully, researchers are advising instructors to re-consider their teaching methods, and to move from a more traditional lecture-based pedagogy to a more facilitative style that encourages student interaction, and a more collaborative, high involvement environment (e.g., Berger, 1999; Arbaugh, 2000a; 2000b; Volery & Lord, 2000). Developing a collaborative and high involvement environment in an online class can help to compensate for the lack of common physical space and face-to-face interaction that a live classroom provides, and help both students and instructors to feel more socially connected–whether the class is synchronous, asynchronous, or some combination.

The idea of a high-involvement class environment may be more familiar to those who teach courses like international management, particularly in terms of using experiential exercises to help students to develop contextual understanding of issues such as cultural diversity. Nevertheless, it is often difficult and sometimes impossible to successfully transfer experiential exercises from a live classroom to an online class environment. Therefore, international business instructors may need to re-think their approach to experiential learning for the online classroom.

At the same time (and regardless of the type of classroom environment), both business curriculum experts and employers cite the need for more emphasis on helping students to enhance communication skills and build contextual understanding–which can be accomplished through experiential, high involvement class environments. According to Day and Glick (2000), curriculum experts express the need for greater development of communication skills, and awareness of cultural differences. Correspondingly, human resources managers indicate that new employees need to have skills including communication and listening skills, team building skills, and understanding of international diversity issues.

Therefore, to address the demands of the online environment, as well as the recommendations by curriculum experts and employers, this paper proposes the use of literature to develop experiential exercises for online classrooms. The value of using literature in the business curriculum has been established (e.g., Puffer, 1991; Harrison and Akinc, 2000), as has the value of using literature in international business (Carney, 1994). Correspondingly, the American Assembly of Collegiate Schools of Business (AACSB) has always maintained that management education must be built on a strong liberal arts foundation (Harrison and Akinc, 2000). However, the purpose of this paper is to make the case for, and to illustrate how literature is a tool that can help instructors to make a successful transition to the online environment.

Use of literature in international management can help students to become better international managers. The complexity and ambiguity inherent in literature can help students to understand and identify with complicated and equivocal international management issues, and helps to develop critical thinking skills. Since literature is not focused exclusively upon the business environment, it allows students the opportunity to leave the traditional business paradigm and "try-on" a new paradigm–in order to return to the business paradigm with new perspectives. According to Winter and McClelland (1981), literature can increase students' capacity to integrate broad ranges of experience and adapt to a new environment when they encounter it. Literature can also help students to develop as a whole person–to see beyond the business environment and into the many other dimensions of the human condition. Therefore, use of literature can address the recommendations by business curriculum experts for development of contextual understanding and awareness of cultural differences.

Likewise, literature can help students to develop a complex understanding of international diversity issues that are valued by employers. According to Harrison and Akinc (2000), as the corporate world becomes increasingly complex and dynamic, a program that integrates the arts and literature into management education will benefit managers at all levels.

Unlike some experiential tools that must be used in a live or synchronous environment, literature can also be used effectively in an asynchronous environment. That is, the use of literature (e.g., short story; folktale; novel chapter, etc.) as the backbone of an experiential exercise allows students to read and react at a time that is convenient for them. In addition, using literature in an online course helps to set the tone of the course as contemplative and integrative, and helps to fight the misperception by some that online courses necessarily lack rigor, and are of lower quality than live courses. Development of a team-oriented assignment based on the assigned literature (as is recommended and explained later in the paper) that requires both informal online discussion between and among students and instructor, and formal written team assignments, can help to enhance students' team and communication skills. Hence, literature may be a valuable tool in helping to adapt teaching methods to the online environment, and in helping to develop and enhance critical skills among students.

To provide a specific example, this paper will explain how the folktale, "Stone Soup," can be used as an introductory exercise that experientially reveals the essence of effective international management. This folktale is particularly well-suited for the first day or week of class, since it can provide students with situational reinforcement of the importance of sensitivity to different cultures, and communication, motivation, leadership, and team building in a different culture.

In addition, "Stone Soup" elicits a high level of student participation and helps to set the standard for high involvement at the start of the course. Initially, the folktale *seems* unrelated to the world of business and international management, so that students who feel that they are lacking in business knowledge or experience are less inhibited about participating. However, the discussion of "Stone Soup" helps to make students aware that international management issues reach far beyond the traditional business world. (Since "Stone Soup" presents an overall view of international management skills and topics, the tale can be used, if desired, as a unifying theme for the whole course; hence, the tale can be revisited when the class focuses on each relevant topic. However, this is not necessary and the tale is also effective as a one-time, stand-alone exercise.) While the focus of this paper is online applications, "Stone Soup" (as well as other forms of literature) can also be used successfully in a live course, or in a course with both live and online components.

The paper is divided into three parts. The first part is a brief description of the folktale, "Stone Soup." The second part describes how to conduct the introductory exercise, and includes some possible approaches for class discussion and variations. The last part is a general discussion and conclusion.

A BRIEF SUMMARY OF "STONE SOUP"

"Stone Soup" is a folktale that exists in several versions. This particular summary is based on the version by Brown (1986). Typically, the story takes place in the past, and is about a small group of tired, hungry soldiers from a far away land who are marching home after the wars.

Along their way, they pass through a village, and politely ask the villagers if they can spare a bit to eat, and a place to sleep for the night. However, the villagers are fearful of soldiers–especially strange soldiers from a strange land. They hide all of their food in their cellars and hay lofts, and tell the soldiers that they had a bad harvest, and have neither food nor spare beds. At this point, the soldiers speak to the villagers with great respect and say, "Since you have no food and are hungry, and we have no food and are hungry, we must make stone soup. All we will need is a fire, a large kettle of water, and three large stones."

The villagers are intrigued, and so they build a fire and set a large kettle of water over it. Then, they add three stones. The soldiers comment on how those particular stones will make a good soup, but politely add that the soup would be so much better with a bit of salt and pepper–and one of the villagers fetches their salt and pepper. As the soldiers shake the salt and pepper into the soup, they comment on how much better the soup will be with a few carrots–and another villager fetches some carrots for the soup. And so it goes, with the soldiers politely commenting on how much better the soup would be with the addition of every conceivable soup ingredient (potatoes, cabbage, milk, a bit of beef, etc.) and the villagers willingly contributing their food to the soup. All the while, the villagers marvel about the soup that is made "just from stones."

When the soup is finished, the soldiers suggest that the villagers set tables in the village square so everyone can enjoy it–and this results in a great celebration that includes singing and dancing, and is better than any other celebration that the village has ever had. Afterward, the soldiers are housed in the best rooms in the village, and are sent off as heroes the next morning. The story ends with the villagers saying to the soldiers, "Many thanks for what you have taught us. We will never go hungry now that we can make soup from stones." The soldiers reply, "Oh, it's all in the knowing how."

Hence, the story is full of opportunities to talk about diversity issues, and how managers and individuals can approach communication, trust building, team building, motivation, leadership, etc., in a diverse, global context.

USING "STONE SOUP" IN AN ONLINE EXERCISE

Probably the quickest and easiest way to allow students to gain access to "Stone Soup" is to assign it as a required text. (A few summaries of the tale are available on the Internet, but since they are summaries, and lack illustrations, they are much less rich than an original version of "Stone Soup.") A version of the tale that is easily available through online or physical bookstores (and works well in international management) is the one by Brown (1986). The story takes about 10-15 minutes to read, so that instructors can assign it as early in the semester as desired (e.g., the first day).

"Stone Soup" can work as an introductory exercise in both undergraduate and graduate international management classes, although different class levels and student experience levels can demand different approaches, and will result in somewhat different topics during class discussion. In many years of teaching, "Stone Soup" has worked consistently well as an introductory exercise–it facilitates high levels of participation and positive team dynamics on the first day of class, which sets the tone for a high involvement environment for the rest of the semester.

"Stone Soup" works rather insidiously on a group of strangers who are taking a course together. At first, its simplicity and *seeming* non-business focus draws in even students who lack confidence about their international management knowledge. Then, it helps all students to realize that international management issues and situations reach far beyond the traditional business world.

Typically, I introduce "Stone Soup" as a non-traditional case in international management (e.g., different than the latest Harvard case). In graduate classes, where we discuss the notion of paradigms, and the need to try-on different paradigms in order to gain new perspectives about our own paradigm, I introduce it as an international management case from a different paradigm. The next section, Discussing the Exercise, will provide some examples of different directions and levels of class discussions.

To facilitate a high involvement environment and communication and team skills, the exercise should be used in a team environment–in the case of a very small class, perhaps the instructor can treat the whole class as one team. Since this exercise is typically done at the start of the course, the instructor can assign teams. The exercise is more powerful and team discussion is more fruitful if there is some diversity among team members (e.g., gender, major, employer, home country, etc.). To facilitate high involvement by team members, the instructor can set up secure chat rooms and/or threaded discussions for each team so that only team members and the instructor have access. The instructor can also limit his/her access, if they choose, in order to allow team members some privacy.

Individual students can read "Stone Soup" at their convenience. Then, individual students and teams are required to informally post and respond to comments about the tale (and/or participate in a live chat, if there is a synchronous portion of the class). Individual students and teams are also required to provide formal, written responses to instructor-generated questions. The instructor-generated questions can guide (or at least initiate) both informal and formal responses. Some sample questions (and responses, as well as ideas for discussion topics) are provided in the next section. These sample questions and responses illustrate how students can use "Stone Soup" to: (1) enhance their contextual understanding of international management issues such as cultural differences; and (2) enhance their communication and team skills. Of course, instructors can adjust the assignment requirements to match their own course requirements.

While the focus of this paper is not how to manage online interaction (e.g., see Berger, 1999; Brindle and Levesque, 2000), the success of this exercise depends upon successful communication between and among several stakeholders (e.g., between individual teams and instructor and vice versa; between individual students and instructors and vice versa; among all class members, etc.). Therefore, instructors need to be clear about communication expectations for individuals and teams, and how all forms of online communication will be rewarded. Before the deadline for formal responses to questions, instructors should encourage and reward questions, comments, and draft answers from teams and/or individuals.

Depending upon the course requirements, the instructor can request formal, written responses from teams only, or from both teams and individuals–the latter requirement can act as a deterrent to free riders and helps to chronicle the learning process for both instructor and students. The requirement of an integrated team answer will facilitate a collaborative, high involvement class environment and enable first-hand experience with team dynamics and conflict management–which can be revisited later in the course. (In the case of a completely asynchronous environment with video-streaming capabilities, the instructor might offer a video presentation, including a reading of "Stone Soup," as well as some additional perspectives and feedback to the class. This can help the instructor to "connect" with the class. Of course, the video-streaming could also be used in a class with an synchronous component, as well.)

Below is a list of potential questions for "Stone Soup," as well as answers and discussion topics that have been offered in the past. The questions, answers, and discussion topics are based on experience in using "Stone Soup" in both undergraduate and graduate classes. Of course, there are no correct answers, and the questions and discussion topics are intended only as suggestions–instructors can construct questions that are appropriate to their own courses. All questions can be distributed to all teams, or questions can be divided among teams:

1. In the beginning of the story, why might the villagers have been afraid of the soldiers?
2. At the end of the story, were the villagers still afraid of the soldiers? Why or why not?
3. Do you think that the soldiers stole from or swindled the villagers? Why or why not?
4. At the end of the story, the villagers said to the soldiers, "Many thanks for what you have taught us." What did the soldiers teach the villagers?
5. Have you ever been in a situation where you felt like the soldiers at the beginning of the story? Or, have you ever known anyone who has been in such a situation? What did you (or they) do? How did things turn out?
6. Does "Stone Soup" teach us anything about international management, or about being an effective international manager?

Discussing the Exercise

This section provides just a few of the possible ways that students and instructors may address the above questions about "Stone Soup" in an introductory exercise in international management. As the possible answers and discussion topics indicate below, instructors and students can use the exercise for a more general, or more in-depth exploration of issues in international management. The questions, topics, and depth of discussion can be adjusted to meet individual class requirements. The level of answers will depend upon the level and experience of the class. The questions are designed to help students to experientially develop contextual understanding of cultural differences and diversity issues that are such a large part of international management. In developing formal, written, answers to the questions, students and teams will enhance team building skills, formal written communication skills, and less formal online (e.g., email) communication skills.

Question 1: In the beginning of the story, why might the villagers have been afraid of the soldiers?

Most students and student teams discuss the fact that the soldiers were different people from a different land, as well as the idea of fear of differences (e.g., different appearance; different speech; different customs; etc.). Since most students have already had an introductory management course, the class can review the concept of culture, and/or the instructor can preview how the course will address culture and cultural diversity. In addition, many students make the point that the soldiers are asking for something–food and shelter. In addition, some students also mention that the soldiers may be feared due to a negative stereotype about soldiers, in general–and because soldiers are often armed. At this point, the class can briefly discuss and/or preview the idea of stereotypes, as it applies to cultural diversity.

Question 2: At the end of the story, were the villagers still afraid of the soldiers? Why or why not?

Most students answer "no," because the soldiers taught the villagers a valuable skill (how to make stone soup), and proved they were trustworthy. Some of the more experienced students acknowledge how the soldiers treated the villagers with respect, and as equals. While the soldiers might have been able to take or get (through threats or intimidation) the food and shelter that they needed, they chose to respect the villagers and their differences. What's more, the soldiers chose to help the villagers by teaching them a skill–how to make stone soup. Therefore, the soldiers helped themselves to achieve their own goals, while also helping everyone else. At this point, the class can briefly discuss topics such as trust-building and respect in a global environment and/or among different cultures.

Question 3: Do you think that the soldiers stole from or swindled the villagers? Why or why not?

This is always an interesting question–some team members say yes; some say absolutely not; some prefer to use the word "trick," rather than swindle. The ones who say no typically argue that the villagers contributed the ingredients willingly–and the villagers received a share in the stone soup that resulted. Most often, the teams' group answers indicate that the soldiers got the villagers to do something that they originally thought they did not want to do, but in the end, was in the villagers' best interest to have done. While discussing this question, some of the more experienced students will say that the soldiers behaved like good managers, since they were able to get people to work together on a project that they originally did not want to participate in, and the project resulted in an outcome that was good for both soldiers and villagers (or managers and employees). At this point, the class can briefly discuss topics such as motivation, leadership, and compensation in international management.

Question 4: At the end of the story, the villagers said to the soldiers, "Many thanks for what you have taught us." What did the soldiers teach the villagers?

Another interesting question–most students and teams will discuss how the soldiers taught the villagers to work as a team, and how teamwork is more productive than individual work. Some more experienced students will talk about how the soldiers taught the villagers a skill that the villagers could perform even after the soldiers were gone–and how the soldiers improved the quality of life for the villagers. At this point, the class can briefly discuss topics such as the importance of teamwork, synergy, and empowerment in order to perform complex tasks.

Question 5: Have you ever been in a situation where you felt like the soldiers at the beginning of the story? Or, have you ever known anyone who has been in such a situation? How did the situation turn out?

Regardless of the answers, this question and corresponding discussion is intended to help students to see the parallels between how the soldiers interacted with the villagers and how international managers might interact with employees in modern organizations. More experienced students may have made this connection earlier in the discussion. More experienced students also sometimes compare the situation of the soldiers and the villagers to that of a brand new managers and his/her new employees–especially when the manager and employees are somehow different (e.g., cultures; background; ages; etc.). Since it is natural for employees to be at least a bit apprehensive about a new manager, the manager must show respect for the employees and their different cultures or backgrounds–and, much like the soldiers, must use a style that will win over the employees, rather than alienate them. In a class of less experienced students, the instructor can more directly guide the discussion to help students to see the parallels between soldiers/villagers and new managers/employees (e.g., Can you see any relationships between the soldiers' behavior with the villagers and that of a new manager with his/her employees?)

Question 6: Does "Stone Soup" have anything in common with international management?

This question typically initiates or continues the analogy between the soldiers/villagers and managers/employees. Students talk about the importance of treating all people (e.g., all cultures; all organization levels; all ages; all genders; etc.) with respect, and as equals–as did the soldiers. More experienced students discuss the importance of building trust and understanding between employees and managers; many observe that without trust, employees will hide their resources (e.g., skills, information, etc.) from the manager–just as the villagers hid their food from the soldiers due to a lack of trust and understanding. Students point out that it is also vital for international managers to empower their employees and to train them to function as an independent team (as much as possible)–as the soldiers trained the villagers to function as an independent team that could make stone soup in the soldiers' absence. At this point, if the students have not introduced it, the instructor can introduce the importance of understanding, respect, trust, and empowerment in the flatter global organizations of the 21st Century.

DISCUSSION AND CONCLUSIONS

The "Stone Soup" exercise is extremely successful in getting almost all members of the class involved in discussion during the first day (or week) of class. The team orientation of the exercise also introduces and sets the tone for a collaborative and high involvement class environment, which is important to the success of any online course. At the end of the course, when I ask students (both undergraduates and graduates) to list what topics, assignments, or exercises helped them to better understand the challenges of management and being a manager, "Stone Soup" is on most lists. Often, students refer to "Stone Soup" in papers and final exam questions.

As illustrated by some of the questions and typical discussion topics in the section above, use of "Stone Soup" allows students to experience and learn about cultural diversity and international management from a non-business paradigm–within the context of a folktale, and to apply what they have learned to better understand international management. Therefore, students are gaining a contextual understanding of critical topics in international management. The team structure of the assignment allows students to experience and learn first-hand about group dynamics and conflict management. The assignment itself (requirement of informal comments and formal written feedback from individuals and teams) allows students to enhance their formal written and less formal written (e.g., email) communication skills.

In addition, experiential exercises that use literature can be easily integrated into online classes–and they can be used to develop contextual understanding and enhance communication and team skills even in asynchronous environments. Experiential exercises that use literature also enhance the rigor of the course, and dispel the misperception that online courses are necessarily of lower quality than live courses.

"Stone Soup" is only one example of how literature can be used in international management. If it is desirable, the instructor can use a series of short stories throughout the course (e.g., Puffer, 1991). As technological capabilities increase, other genres (e.g., film) can also be used to train more effective international managers in an online environment.

Hence, literature may be one tool that helps us to make a smooth transition to the online teaching environment in international management–and the purpose of this paper was to make this case, and to illustrate how it might be done. The next step in this research, and therefore, the focus of the next paper on this topic, needs to be empirical assessment of the effectiveness of literature in online classrooms relative to live classrooms.

REFERENCES

Arbaugh, J. (2000a). Virtual Classroom Characteristics and Student Satisfaction with Internet-Based MBA Courses. *Journal of Management Education*, 24(1): 32-54.

Arbaugh, J. (2000b). Virtual Classroom Versus Physical Classroom: An Exploratory Study of Class Discussion Patterns and Student Learning in an Asynchronous Internet-Based MBA Course. *Journal of Management Education*, 24(2): 213-33.

Berger, N. (1999). Pioneering Experiences in Distance Learning: Lessons Learned. *Journal of Management Education*, 23(6): 684-90.

Brown, M. *Stone Soup*. (1986). New York: Macmillan Publishing Company.

Brindle, M. and Levesque, L. (2000). Bridging the Gap: Challenges and Prescriptions for Interactive Distance Education. *Journal of Management Education*, 24(4): 445-57.

Carney, C. (1994). Making Fiction Integrative: The Role of Literature in the International Business Curriculum. Paper presented at the Annual Eastern Michigan University Conference on Language and Communication for World Business and the Professions, April 14-16, 16 pp.

Day, N. and Glick, B. (2000). Teaching Diversity: A Study of Organizational Needs and Diversity Curriculum in Higher Education. *Journal of Management Education*, 24(3): 338-52.

Harrison, J. and Akinc, H. (2000). Lessons in Leadership from the Arts and Literature: A Liberal Arts Approach to Management Education Through Fifth Discipline Learning. *Journal of Management Education*, 24(3): 391-413.

Puffer, S. (1991). *Managerial Insights from Literature*. Boston: PWS-Kent.

Shrivastava, P. (1999). Management Classes as Online Learning Communities. *Journal of Management Education*, 23(6): 691-702.

Volery, T. and Lord, D. (2000). Critical Success Factors in Online Education. *The International Journal of Educational Management*, 14(5).

Winter, D.; McClelland, D.; and Stewart, A. (1981). *A New Case for the Liberal Arts: Assessing Institutional Goals and Student Development*. San Francisco: Jossey-Bass.

Index

